Food Manager Certification Study Guide

TABLE OF CONTENTS

Dear Reader,

Thank you for picking up the "Food Manager Certification Study Guide." By choosing this book, you're not just investing in your career — you're showing your commitment to food safety and to excelling in the food service world.

I've poured my expertise and passion for food safety into this book, crafting it into a user-friendly and effective manual. It will provide you with the knowledge and skills you need to achieve your food manager certification. I believe that with the right tools and determination, you can achieve your certification and make a positive impact on the food industry.

I love to hear about success stories, so if you found this guide a valuable resource on your path to certification, could you please leave a review on Amazon.com? Your thoughts mean a lot to me and could help other food industry hopefuls like you on their journey to success.

And as a thank you for your feedback, I've created a bonus eBook packed with 150 practice tests. These tests are designed to help prepare you thoroughly and are your secret weapon for acing that certification exam. You can find the link and QR code to unlock this exclusive eBook at the back of this study guide.

Thanks again for choosing the "Food Manager Certification Study Guide." Here's to your future success as a certified food manager!

Ray K. Firth

Introduction to the Food Manager Certification Exam in the USA

The United States, with its vast culinary landscape, diverse population, and booming food service industry, necessitates a rigorous and standardized system of ensuring that the individuals overseeing food operations maintain the highest standards of food safety and hygiene. This pivotal responsibility is entrusted to food managers, who are often required to be certified. The Food Manager Certification is proof that the individual has acquired the necessary knowledge and skills to ensure that food is stored, prepared, and served in a safe manner, minimizing the risk of foodborne illnesses.

1. The Rationale Behind the Certification:
Before delving into the specifics of the exam, it's crucial to understand its importance. With millions of cases of foodborne illnesses reported annually, having certified food managers in establishments is not just a regulatory requirement in many states but also a critical public health strategy. The certification process is designed to ensure that these professionals are equipped with the most recent knowledge on food safety practices, guidelines, and regulations.

2. Who Should Take the Exam?
Individuals seeking managerial positions in the foodservice sector, including restaurants, cafeterias, and food trucks, should consider obtaining this certification. Additionally, those in related sectors, such as food manufacturing or distribution, can benefit from the knowledge and credibility that come with being certified.

3. Exam Providers and Accreditation:
While the specifics of the Food Manager Certification can vary from state to state, several accredited exam providers offer the certification at a national level. Two of the primary bodies are the ServSafe Food Protection Manager Certification Examination and the Food Safety Manager Certification Examination (FSMCE). These exams are accredited by the American National Standards Institute (ANSI) and the Conference for Food Protection (CFP).

4. Exam Format and Content:

Typically, the Food Manager Certification Exam tests candidates on a range of topics that span the entire food production and service process. These topics can include, but are not limited to:

- Basics of food safety and hygiene.
- Personal hygiene standards and practices.
- Purchasing, receiving, and storage procedures.
- Safe food preparation and serving techniques.
- Cleaning and sanitization.
- Pest control and management.
- Understanding of foodborne pathogens, illnesses, and allergens.
- Crisis management in cases of suspected food contamination.
- Regulatory guidelines and compliance.
- The exam often comprises multiple-choice questions, and the duration can vary, but most tests take between 1.5 to 2 hours to complete. A passing grade, generally 70% or higher, signifies that the candidate possesses the knowledge required to manage food safety in a professional setting.

5. Preparing for the Exam:

Given the comprehensive nature of the certification exam, preparation is essential. Many providers offer study materials, including textbooks, practice exams, and even courses. These resources cover critical food safety concepts, laws, and best practices. Enrolling in a preparatory course, whether online or in-person, can offer structured learning and expert guidance, increasing the chances of passing the exam on the first attempt.

6. Certification Validity and Renewal:

Once obtained, the Food Manager Certification typically remains valid for a period of three to five years, after which it must be renewed. The renewal often involves retaking the exam, ensuring that certified professionals stay updated on the latest in food safety standards and practices.

7. State-Specific Requirements:

While many states recognize the certifications from major accredited providers, it's essential to research the specific requirements of the state where one plans to work. Some states might have additional prerequisites or might mandate training before attempting the exam.

8. Benefits of Certification:

Beyond fulfilling a legal requirement in many states, the certification offers numerous benefits. For establishments, having certified managers can reduce the risk of food safety incidents, positively impacting their reputation and bottom line. For individuals, the certification can enhance employability, pave the way for career advancement, and instill a genuine understanding of the significant responsibility they hold in ensuring public health.

9. Registration and Eligibility:

Before registering for the Food Manager Certification Exam, it's essential to check if there are any prerequisites. Some states or exam providers may require candidates to have completed a certain number of hours in food service or have undergone prior food safety training. Registration can typically be done online through the exam provider's website, and there might be a fee associated with the test.

10. Test Centers and Online Proctoring:

The Food Manager Certification Exam can be taken at approved test centers located throughout the country. These centers are equipped with the necessary facilities to ensure a smooth examination process. In recent years, with the advent of technology, some providers have started offering online proctored exams. This allows candidates to take the exam from the comfort of their homes while being monitored via webcam to maintain the test's integrity.

11. Accommodations for Special Needs:

Recognizing the diverse needs of candidates, many exam providers offer accommodations for those with disabilities or special requirements. This can include extended time, separate testing rooms, or the provision of a reader or scribe. It's important to notify the test provider well in advance and provide necessary documentation to avail of these accommodations.

12. Re-examination and Appeals:

For those who do not pass the exam on their first attempt, most providers allow for re-examination. However, there might be a waiting period before the test can be retaken. Furthermore, if a candidate feels that there was an error in scoring or that the testing conditions were not adequate, they can usually appeal to the exam provider. This process might involve a review of the test or a re-examination under monitored conditions.

13. Staying Updated Post-Certification:

Once certified, it's essential for food managers to stay abreast of changes in food safety regulations, guidelines, and best practices. Subscribing to industry newsletters, joining professional associations, or attending workshops and seminars can be beneficial. Many states or local health departments also periodically release updates and bulletins relevant to the food service industry.

14. Ethical Considerations:

The Food Manager Certification is not just about knowledge; it's also about upholding a certain standard of ethical conduct. Certified individuals are expected to prioritize public health and safety over any commercial interests. Any breach of this trust, such as knowingly serving compromised food or violating safety protocols, can result in severe consequences, including revocation of the certification.

15. Career Progression and Advanced Certifications:

While the Food Manager Certification is foundational, there are additional certifications and courses available for those looking to specialize further. For instance, there are certifications focusing solely on seafood safety, bakery operations, or international cuisines. Pursuing these can open doors to specialized roles within the food industry or even consultancy positions.

Below you will find a concise overview for each state regarding the Food Manager Certification Exam.

Alabama: The Alabama Department of Public Health requires at least one manager in each food service establishment to have a food safety certification from an accredited program.

Alaska: Alaska requires a certified Food Protection Manager (CFPM) in most food establishments. The state provides a list of approved exams.

Arizona: Arizona leaves the certification requirements up to individual counties, but most require at least one CFPM per establishment.

Arkansas: The Arkansas Department of Health requires a certified food protection manager on-site during all hours of operation for most establishments.

California: All food facilities that prepare, handle, or serve non-prepackaged potentially hazardous food must have at least one certified food manager.

Colorado: While Colorado does not have a statewide requirement, individual counties may require food protection manager certification.

Connecticut: At least one certified food operator is required in most food establishments.

Delaware: Delaware requires one CFPM on-site when food is being prepared. This includes all shifts.

Florida: Florida requires each establishment to have a certified food manager. Certifications are granted after passing an ANSI-accredited Food Protection Manager Certification program.

Georgia: All food service establishments must have at least one CFPM.

Hawaii: High-risk establishments in Hawaii require a CFPM. The state accepts certifications from ANSI-accredited programs.

Idaho: Most food establishments need a Food Protection Manager Certification, accepting certificates from any Conference for Food Protection-recognized program.

Illinois: Each establishment is required to have at least one certified food protection manager. Recognized exams include ServSafe.

Indiana: Every establishment must have one certified food manager, with slight variations possibly at the county level.

Iowa: A current certification is required for at least one food protection manager in food establishments.

Kansas: While no statewide requirement exists, individual counties or cities might have one.

Kentucky: All food establishments need a certified food manager on-site. The certification test must be state-approved.

Louisiana: Every retail food establishment requires a CFPM. The Department of Health provides an approved list.

Maine: A certified food protection manager is a must for all eating establishments.

Maryland: Food service facilities need a certified food manager present during all operational hours.

Massachusetts: At least one full-time certified food protection manager is mandatory for food establishments, using an approved program.

Michigan: A certified manager or operator is essential for every food establishment.

Minnesota: A certified food manager is a requirement for all food establishments, barring specific exemptions.

Mississippi: Most retail food establishments must have at least one manager with a food manager certification. The state provides a list of approved training programs.

Missouri: The requirements vary by county, but many require food establishments to have a certified food protection manager.

Montana: Montana requires a certified food protection manager at establishments, depending on the risk level. High-risk establishments typically need a CFPM.

Nebraska: Every food establishment must have at least one person who has completed a food safety certification program.

Nevada: In Nevada, particularly in counties like Clark County (which includes Las Vegas), a certified food safety manager must be on duty at all times.

New Hampshire: Most food service establishments need at least one CFPM on the premises during operational hours.

New Jersey: There is no state-wide CFPM requirement, but individual counties might have specific requirements.

New Mexico: Each food establishment should have at least one CFPM. This is typically based on the risk of the food service operation.

New York: While the state does not have a uniform requirement, cities like New York City require food establishments to have at least one certified food protection manager.

North Carolina: Food establishments must employ at least one CFPM who has passed an ANSI-accredited exam.

North Dakota: High-risk food establishments typically require a CFPM, though this can vary based on local jurisdiction.

Ohio: Most food service operations and retail food establishments require at least one CFPM, as per the Ohio Department of Health.

Oklahoma: Food establishments are required to have a minimum of one certified food manager. The certification must be recognized by the Oklahoma Department of Health.

Oregon: Oregon requires a CFPM for most food establishments, especially those deemed high risk.

Pennsylvania: While there is no state-wide requirement, many counties, including major cities like Philadelphia, mandate food safety certification.

Rhode Island: Every food establishment is required to have a manager certified in food safety.

South Carolina: The Department of Health and Environmental Control necessitates at least one certified food protection manager on-site.

South Dakota: All licensed food service and food processing establishments must have a certified food service manager.

Tennessee: Every establishment must have a certified manager present during all hours of operation.

Texas: All food establishments need to have a certified food manager present during hours of operation. Texas has its own certification program but also recognizes ANSI-accredited programs.

Utah: Utah requires food establishments to have at least one CFPM. The certification must be renewed every three years.

Vermont: Vermont mandates at least one CFPM in higher-risk food establishments.

Virginia: While there's no state-wide requirement, specific localities may require CFPMs based on the risk associated with the establishment.

Washington: The Washington State Department of Health requires at least one CFPM in most food establishments.

West Virginia: Food establishments should have at least one certified manager. Local health departments may have additional requirements.

Wisconsin: Food establishments must have at least one licensed and certified food manager.

Wyoming: While there's no state-wide mandate, local jurisdictions might have specific requirements for CFPMs based on the risk of the establishment.

It's important to note that while the above are general guidelines, local counties or municipalities within a state can have their additional requirements or variations to the state guidelines. Some states might have reciprocity with others, meaning they recognize certifications obtained in another state. Still, this isn't universal, so it's essential always to check the specific requirements of each state and even county.

Lastly, the specifics of the exam, including the number of questions, passing score, cost, and retake policies, might vary depending on the provider and state. While many states recognize exams from institutions accredited by the American National Standards Institute (ANSI) and the Conference for Food Protection (CFP), always ensure that your chosen certification is accepted in the state where you plan to work.

For a comprehensive overview of each state, detailed research and collaboration with state health departments would be required. This short guide serves as a starting point and for more exhaustive information, always refer to the specific health department or regulatory body of each state.

Chapter 1: Foodborne Microorganisms & Allergens

1.1 Introduction to Foodborne Microorganisms

When we refer to 'foodborne microorganisms,' we are discussing a diverse group of microscopic organisms capable of causing illness when ingested with food. These organisms primarily consist of bacteria, viruses, and parasites, and they are sometimes collectively termed "pathogens." Understanding the nature, behavior, and impact of these microorganisms is crucial for anyone involved in food handling, preparation, and service.

Defining the Microorganisms

1. **Bacteria**: These are single-celled microorganisms that thrive in various environments, from extreme heat to freezing conditions. While many bacteria are beneficial, aiding in processes like fermentation or digestion, certain strains can be harmful and lead to foodborne illnesses. Examples include Salmonella, E. coli, and Listeria monocytogenes.

2. **Viruses:** Unlike bacteria, viruses need a host to survive and reproduce. They are much smaller than bacteria and can lead to diseases when they invade living, host cells. The norovirus and hepatitis A are examples of viruses that can be transmitted through contaminated food.

3. **Parasites:** These are organisms that live on or in a host, obtaining nourishment from the host, often at the host's expense. Parasites like Giardia or Cryptosporidium can contaminate food and cause illnesses when ingested.

Significance in the Food Industry

The presence of harmful foodborne microorganisms poses a substantial threat to public health. Every year, millions of people in the United States suffer from foodborne illnesses, leading to thousands of hospitalizations and, sadly, several deaths. These statistics underscore the importance of understanding and controlling these pathogens in our food supply.

Several factors enhance the significance of these microorganisms:

- Economic Impact: Foodborne illness outbreaks can lead to massive recalls, lawsuits, and loss of sales for businesses. The economic repercussions can be dire, particularly for small and medium-sized businesses that might struggle to recover from a tainted reputation.

- Globalization of the Food Supply: As our food supply becomes more globalized, the potential for widespread outbreaks increases. An infected ingredient in one part of the world can affect products in various regions, complicating source tracking and mitigation efforts.

- Vulnerability of At-risk Populations: Certain groups, such as children, the elderly, pregnant women, and immunocompromised individuals, are more susceptible to foodborne illnesses. For these groups, what might be a mild illness in the general population can become severe or even fatal.

- Emergence of New Strains: Microorganisms evolve over time. New strains of bacteria and viruses can emerge, some of which might be more virulent or resistant to traditional treatment methods. Staying informed and updated on these evolving threats is paramount.

1.2 Major Foodborne Microorganisms

The diverse world of foodborne microorganisms includes a range of pathogens that pose a significant risk to public health. To effectively manage and mitigate these risks, it's crucial to understand the primary culprits, their developmental processes, and the consequences of their presence in our food.

Bacteria

1. **Salmonella:** This bacterium is one of the most common causes of food poisoning in the U.S. It's often found in raw poultry, eggs, and unpasteurized milk. When ingested, it can lead to symptoms like diarrhea, fever, and abdominal cramps.

   Salmonella can multiply rapidly at temperatures between 40°F and 140°F (often referred to as the "danger zone"). It's essential to store and cook food at the right temperatures to prevent its growth.

In extreme cases, Salmonella can result in hospitalization or even death, particularly in vulnerable populations.

2. **E. coli:** There are many strains of E. coli, but only a few are harmful. The notorious O157:H7 strain, often found in raw or undercooked ground beef, can lead to severe abdominal cramps, bloody diarrhea, and vomiting.

Like Salmonella, E. coli thrives in the danger zone. It can also survive in acidic environments, making it a particular concern in products like unpasteurized apple cider.

In some instances, infections can lead to a life-threatening condition called hemolytic uremic syndrome (HUS), especially in children.

3. **Listeria monocytogenes**: Found in soil and water, Listeria can contaminate a variety of foods. Unlike many bacteria, it can grow even in cold temperatures, like those of a refrigerator.

Listeria is hardy and can grow in acidic, salty, and cold environments. Ready-to-eat foods, like deli meats, can be at risk.

Infections can lead to listeriosis, a severe disease that can be fatal, especially for pregnant women, the elderly, and immunocompromised individuals.

Viruses

1. **Norovirus**: Often dubbed the "stomach flu," this virus is highly contagious. It can be transmitted through contaminated food, surfaces, or direct contact with an infected person.

Norovirus does not grow in food like bacteria, but it can survive on foods and surfaces, waiting to infect a host.

Norovirus causes acute gastrointestinal symptoms, leading to dehydration and, in rare cases, death.

2. **Hepatitis A:** This liver-affecting virus can be transmitted through food or water contaminated by small amounts of stool from an infected person.

Hepatitis A is able to survive outside a body for several months. Shellfish from contaminated waters or foods handled by an infected person are common sources.

While many cases are mild, Hepatitis A can cause severe liver problems and is especially dangerous for older adults and those with other liver diseases.

Parasites

1. **Giardia:** A microscopic parasite that can live in the intestines of people and animals. It's found in soil, food, or water contaminated by feces from an infected host.

Giardia forms hardy cysts that can survive outside a host for long periods, waiting to infect a new host.

Causes giardiasis, leading to diarrhea, gas, and stomach cramps.

2. **Cryptosporidium:** Another microscopic parasite, this organism is found in every region of the U.S. and throughout the world.

The parasite is protected by an outer shell that allows it to survive outside the body for long periods.

This parasite has an exterior shell that enables its longevity outside the host for long periods.

Causes cryptosporidiosis, a respiratory and gastrointestinal illness.

1.3 Foodborne Illnesses

Foodborne illnesses, often colloquially termed "food poisoning," result from consuming food contaminated with pathogens or toxins. The outcomes can range from mild discomfort to severe health complications, or in extreme cases, death. In this chapter, we'll examine the symptoms of various foodborne illnesses and discuss strategies to prevent them.

Identifying Symptoms of Foodborne Illnesses

Being able to recognize the signs of foodborne illnesses is the first step in effective treatment and reporting. The following are typical symptoms:

- **Digestive Symptoms:** These are the most common and include nausea, vomiting, diarrhea, abdominal pain, and cramps. They often arise within hours of consuming contaminated food.
- **Fever:** Many foodborne pathogens cause a fever as the body attempts to fight off the infection.
- **Muscle Aches**: Some illnesses might lead to generalized muscle pain or weakness.
- **Neurological Symptoms**: In cases of contamination by certain toxins, neurological symptoms such as blurred vision, tingling in the extremities, dizziness, or paralysis might be observed.
- **Prolonged Symptoms:** While many foodborne illnesses resolve within a couple of days, symptoms that last longer than two or three days or are particularly severe warrant medical attention.

Key Foodborne Illnesses and Their Symptoms

1. **Salmonellosis (caused by Salmonella):**

Symptoms: Diarrhea, fever, abdominal cramps, headache.

Onset: 6 to 48 hours after exposure.

2. **E. coli infection:**

Symptoms: Severe stomach cramps, diarrhea (often bloody), vomiting.

Onset: 3 to 4 days after exposure.

3. **Listeriosis (caused by Listeria):**

Symptoms: Fever, muscle aches, diarrhea, headache, stiff neck, confusion, loss of balance.

Onset: Can range from a few days to a few weeks after exposure.

4. **Norovirus infection:**

Symptoms: Diarrhea, vomiting, nausea, stomach pain.

Onset: 12 to 48 hours after exposure.

5. **Hepatitis A infection:**

Symptoms: Fatigue, sudden nausea and vomiting, abdominal pain, loss of appetite, jaundice.

Onset: 15 to 50 days after exposure.

6. **Giardiasis (caused by Giardia):**

Symptoms: Diarrhea, gas, stomach cramps, dehydration.

Onset: 1 to 3 weeks after exposure.

Prevention Strategies

Effective prevention is the cornerstone of reducing the incidence of food-borne illnesses. The following strategies are paramount:

1. **Practice Good Personal Hygiene**:

Always wash hands with soap and water for at least 20 seconds before handling food and after using the restroom, coughing, sneezing, or handling raw meat.

2. **Safe Food Handling and Preparation:**

Separate raw and cooked foods.

Use a food thermometer to ensure foods reach safe internal temperatures.

Do not consume foods past their expiration dates.

3. **Proper Food Storage:**

Refrigerate perishable foods promptly.

Ensure refrigerators operate at or below 40°F and freezers at 0°F.

Regularly check stored foods for signs of spoilage.

4. **Educate and Train Staff:**

Provide food safety training for all employees handling food.

Emphasize the importance of reporting illnesses and not working when sick.

5. **Regular Cleaning and Sanitization:**

Clean and sanitize all surfaces and utensils used for food preparation.

Ensure cleaning agents are suitable for food environments.

6. **Safe Water and Raw Materials:**

Use treated water for food preparation.

Purchase raw materials from trusted and reputable sources.

1.4 Common Food Allergens

In the realm of food safety, allergens present a unique challenge. Unlike pathogens, which can be eliminated or reduced to safe levels, allergens are naturally occurring substances in foods. For individuals with food allergies, exposure to even a minuscule amount of the allergenic substance can trigger severe, potentially life-threatening reactions. Thus, proper identification and management of food allergens are of utmost importance in the food industry.

Identifying Common Food Allergens

There are countless allergenic substances in the food world, but a select few are responsible for the majority of allergic reactions. These are often referred to as the "Big Eight" allergens:

1. **Milk**: Not to be confused with lactose intolerance, a milk allergy is an immune response to the proteins found in milk, primarily casein and whey.

2. **Eggs:** Both the white and the yolk can contain allergenic proteins, but the white is more often the culprit.

3. **Peanuts:** These are legumes and are different from tree nuts. Peanut allergies can be particularly severe, with reactions sometimes triggered by very tiny amounts.

4. **Tree Nuts:** This category includes almonds, cashews, walnuts, and several others. It's possible for someone to be allergic to one type of tree nut and not others, though caution is often recommended due to cross-contamination risks.

5. **Soy:** Found in a variety of food products, from tofu to certain baked goods, soy is a versatile ingredient and common allergen.

6. **Wheat:** This allergy is to proteins in wheat and is distinct from celiac disease, an autoimmune condition triggered by gluten, a protein found in wheat, barley, and rye.

7. **Fish:** This category encompasses finned fish like salmon, tuna, and cod. Like tree nuts, an individual might be allergic to one type of fish but not others.

8. **Shellfish:** This includes crustaceans and mollusks, such as shrimp, crab, lobster, oysters, and clams.

Management of Food Allergens

Handling allergens properly is essential to prevent cross-contact and ensure consumer safety. Here are strategies and best practices:

Training and Education:

All staff members should be trained to understand the importance of allergen management.

They should be aware of the "Big Eight" allergens and the foods that contain them.

Ingredient Storage:

Store allergenic foods or ingredients separately from other foods.

Clearly label storage areas and containers to indicate the presence of allergens.

Dedicated Equipment and Utensils:

Where possible, use separate equipment for allergenic and non-allergenic foods.

If shared equipment is used, thorough cleaning and sanitization are vital between uses.

Communication with Customers:

Clearly label menu items or products that contain common allergens.

Train staff to answer questions about ingredients and to communicate allergy concerns to the kitchen.

Preparation Protocols:

Prepare allergen-free dishes first to minimize the risk of cross-contact.

Use separate prep areas, or thoroughly clean surfaces before preparing allergen-free dishes.

Emergency Preparedness:

Train staff to recognize the signs of an allergic reaction: hives, shortness of breath, swelling, dizziness, etc.

Have an emergency protocol in place, including access to an epinephrine auto-injector and knowledge of how to use it.

1.5 Allergen Communication in Food Service

The landscape of food consumption has evolved rapidly, with more people than ever before identifying as having food allergies. For these individuals, dining out can be fraught with anxiety, as the ingestion of even trace amounts of an allergen can lead to severe, sometimes life-threatening reactions. This underscores the importance of effective allergen communication in the food service industry. Proper communication not only helps prevent allergic reactions but also fosters trust with patrons, ensuring they can make informed and safe dining choices.

The Significance of Effective Allergen Communication

- **Consumer Safety:** This is the primary and most crucial reason. Miscommunication or lack of it can lead to severe allergic reactions, which could have legal and ethical implications for the establishment.
- **Building Trust with Patrons:** When customers know that a food establishment takes allergens seriously and communicates effectively, they are more likely to trust and revisit that establishment.
- **Regulatory Compliance:** Many jurisdictions now have regulations or guidelines pertaining to allergen labeling and communication in

food service settings.

- **Reputation Management:** In the age of online reviews and social media, one mishandled allergen incident can significantly damage an establishment's reputation.

Methods of Allergen Communication

1. **Menu Labeling:**

- Clear Indicators: Use symbols or specific fonts to highlight dishes that contain common allergens.
- Dedicated Allergen-Free Menus: Offer separate menus that cater to common allergens, e.g., gluten-free or nut-free menus.

2. **Staff Training:**

- Regular Training Sessions: Ensure all front-of-house and kitchen staff undergo regular training on allergen awareness.
- Role-playing Scenarios: Engage staff in mock scenarios where they handle customer allergen inquiries or potential cross-contact situations.

3. **Verbal Communication:**

- Active Inquiry: Servers should actively ask patrons if they have any food allergies.
- Kitchen Communication: If a patron indicates an allergy, this information should be communicated clearly and immediately to the kitchen staff.

4. **Signage:**

- Table Tents and Posters: Display information about allergens using table tents on dining tables or posters in visible areas.
- At Point-of-Sale: Place reminders for customers to inform staff about any allergies.

5. **Digital and Online Communication:**

- Website Information: Ensure the restaurant's website has a dedicated section on allergens, detailing menu items, preparation practices, and any potential for cross-contact.
- Mobile Apps: If the establishment has a mobile ordering app, include allergen filters and information.

6. **Feedback Mechanisms:**

- Comment Cards and Online Surveys: Provide patrons with the opportunity to give feedback on allergen handling and communication.
- Open Channels for Concerns: Establish a clear channel through which customers can communicate their concerns or incidents related to allergens.

Transparency is Key: always be open and honest with patrons. If there's any doubt about a dish being free from a particular allergen, it's better to err on the side of caution.

Also Ensure that allergen communication practices are consistent across all shifts and staff members and stay updated: as food trends change and new products are introduced, the allergen profile of dishes might change.

Consider collaborating with allergists or dietitians to review menus and preparation practices.

Chapter 2: Personal Hygiene

2.1 The Role of Personal Hygiene in Food Handling

Good personal hygiene can be the frontline defense against the spread of foodborne illnesses, ensuring the health and safety of consumers. This chapter delves into the role of personal hygiene in food handling and elucidates why maintaining high hygiene standards is of utmost significance.

Personal Hygiene: The First Line of Defense

- **Pathogen Transmission**: Food handlers can easily become vectors for the transmission of pathogens. Bacteria, viruses, and other harmful agents can be transferred from one's hands, face, or clothing onto the food, which is then consumed by patrons. Ensuring personal cleanliness minimizes this risk.
- **Trust and Reputation:** An observably clean and hygienic food handler instills confidence in consumers. Conversely, neglect in this area can negatively impact the reputation of an establishment and deter patrons.
- **Regulatory Compliance:** In many jurisdictions, regulatory bodies have set hygiene standards for food handlers. Non-compliance can result in fines, sanctions, or even closure.

Key Components of Personal Hygiene in Food Handling

1. **Hand Hygiene:**

- Handwashing: This is arguably the most critical hygiene practice. Hands should be washed with soap and warm water for at least 20 seconds, especially after using the restroom, before starting work, after handling raw food, and after any activity that contaminates hands.
- Hand Sanitizers: While not a substitute for handwashing, sanitizers

can provide an additional layer of protection.

- Hair Restraints: Hair contains oils, dead skin cells, and can harbor contaminants. Food handlers should always use hair restraints like hair-nets, hats, or scarves.

2. **Clean Clothing and Uniforms:**

Clothing can trap contaminants and transfer them to food. Clean, protective clothing should be worn, and items like aprons should be changed regularly.

3. **Avoiding Touching Face and Hair:** Touching one's face, nose, or hair can transfer pathogens to the hands, which can then be transferred to food.

4. **Personal Health:** Food handlers feeling ill, especially with symptoms like diarrhea, vomiting, jaundice, or fever, should not handle food. Some illnesses can be easily spread to others even before symptoms appear, so awareness and proactive measures are essential.

5. **Wound Care:** Any cuts or wounds on the hands or arms should be properly covered with a waterproof bandage. In many cases, wearing gloves can provide an additional barrier.

6. **Nail Care:** Nails can harbor dirt and pathogens. Food handlers should keep their nails short, clean, and without polish.

Impact of Neglecting Personal Hygiene

- Spread of Foodborne Illnesses: Poor personal hygiene is a leading cause of foodborne outbreaks. Harmful pathogens like E. coli, Salmonella, and norovirus can spread rapidly when food handlers do not practice proper hygiene.
- Economic Consequences: An outbreak traced back to a particular

establishment can lead to loss of business, lawsuits, and significant financial ramifications.

- Loss of Trust: Consumers put their trust in food establishments every time they choose to dine or purchase food. This trust can be irreparably damaged when hygiene standards are not maintained.

2.2 Proper Handwashing Techniques

At the core of hand hygiene is the art and science of handwashing. It's a seemingly simple act, yet when done correctly, its impact is profound.

The hands are the primary tools with which food handlers interact with ingredients, utensils, and finished dishes. Throughout the course of a day, hands come into contact with numerous surfaces, substances, and even pathogens that can't be seen with the naked eye. These microorganisms, when transferred to food, can cause illnesses in those who consume it. Proper handwashing, therefore, serves as a crucial line of defense against such potential contaminations.

It's essential to understand that germs and bacteria are ubiquitous. Not all bacteria are harmful; however, our hands can pick up pathogenic bacteria from various sources, including raw meat, contaminated surfaces, or even after using the restroom. Handwashing helps in significantly reducing the number of these harmful agents.

The Steps of Proper Handwashing

1. Wetting the Hands: Begin by ensuring your hands are completely wet. Use warm water, as it helps in effectively removing oils from the hands that can harbor bacteria. The temperature should be comfortable to avoid scalding.

2. Applying Soap: Once your hands are wet, apply enough soap to cover all hand surfaces. Soap helps lift dirt, grease, and harmful microorganisms from the skin.

3. Lathering and Scrubbing: Rub your hands palm to palm to create a lather. Interlace your fingers and rub them together, ensuring the back of your hands and between your fingers are also well scrubbed. Pay attention to the areas under the nails and the back of the thumb, as these are often overlooked.

4. Duration: The scrubbing should last for at least 20 seconds. A common tip is to hum the "Happy Birthday" song twice to ensure you're washing for the right amount of time.

5. Rinsing: Rinse your hands thoroughly under running water. It's essential to use running water to ensure that the soap and loosened contaminants are washed away completely.

6. Drying: Once rinsed, dry your hands using a clean towel, disposable paper towel, or an air dryer. Drying is a crucial step as germs can transfer more easily to and from wet hands.

7. Turning Off the Tap: If you're using a tap that requires manual shutting, use a tissue or paper towel to turn it off to ensure you don't re-contaminate your hands.

It's imperative to wash your hands:

- Before starting work and after breaks.
- Before handling and preparing food.
- After touching raw food, especially raw meat and poultry.
- After handling waste or taking out the trash.
- After using the restroom.

- After coughing, sneezing, or touching the face.
- After cleaning tasks or handling chemicals.
- Whenever hands are visibly dirty.

2.3 Proper Use of Gloves and Masks

Beyond handwashing, the use of gloves and masks has become an integral component of personal hygiene practices. Both gloves and masks serve as barriers against potential contamination, but their effectiveness is contingent upon proper usage.

The Role of Gloves in Food Handling

Gloves, when used correctly, can prevent the transmission of pathogens from the hands to the food. However, it's crucial to remember that gloves are not a substitute for handwashing. They are an additional layer of protection. Before donning gloves, hands should be cleaned thoroughly.

Different tasks may require different kind of gloves. For instance:

- **Latex Gloves**: While effective, they might not be suitable for food handling due to potential latex allergies.
- **Nitrile or Vinyl Gloves**: These are often preferred in food establishments due to their resistance to punctures and their lack of allergenic properties.

Proper Donning of Gloves

- Ensure Clean Hands: Before putting on gloves, wash hands thoroughly.
- Check for Integrity: Before donning, inspect the gloves for any tears

or holes.

- Size Matters: The glove should fit snugly but not too tight. A glove that's too big can reduce dexterity, while one that's too tight might tear.

Glove Use Recommendations

- Change Regularly: Gloves should be changed frequently, especially between tasks like handling raw meat and ready-to-eat foods.
- Avoid Cross-Contamination: Just as with bare hands, gloved hands should not touch multiple food types without changing gloves to avoid cross-contamination.
- Replace Torn Gloves: If a glove gets torn or damaged during use, it should be replaced immediately.

The Role of Masks in Food Handling

While traditionally masks weren't standard in most food service environments, recent health concerns and events have highlighted their importance in preventing respiratory droplets from contaminating food and surfaces.

You have to select the right type of mask

- **Cloth Masks**: They can be effective for general protection, but they should be cleaned daily.
- **Disposable Masks**: Often made of layers of synthetic materials, they offer protection but should be discarded after a day's use or when visibly soiled or wet.

Proper Donning of Masks

- Clean Hands First: Before touching the mask, ensure hands are clean.

- Ensure Proper Fit: The mask should cover both the nose and mouth. It should fit snugly against the sides of the face without any gaps.

Mask Use Recommendations

- Avoid Touching the Mask: Once the mask is on, try to avoid touching it. If it needs adjusting, ensure hands are cleaned before and after.
- Replace Wet or Soiled Masks: Masks that become damp or soiled should be replaced immediately.
- Correct Removal: Try to take off the mask without touching the front. Dispose of it properly if it's disposable or store appropriately if it's reusable.

2.4 Recommended Attire and Accessories

The attire and accessories chosen by food service professionals play a pivotal role in ensuring both their safety and the hygiene of the food they handle. Every item, from the chef's hat to the server's shoes, serves a purpose in preventing contamination and ensuring a clean and efficient working environment.

The Chef's Uniform

The traditional chef's uniform, often white, is not merely symbolic of culinary artistry; it's also a practical outfit designed to ensure safety and hygiene.

1. Chef's Hat (Toque): Traditionally tall, the chef's hat serves multiple purposes. It prevents hair from falling into the food, absorbs sweat, and denotes the chef's rank in the kitchen.

2. Double-Breasted Jacket: Made of heavy-duty material, the double-breasted design provides an extra layer of protection against hot spills and splatters. Its reversible nature allows a chef to conceal stains if necessary quickly.

3. Pants: Often designed with a loose fit, chef's pants are made to be comfortable and protective. Their patterns, like houndstooth, help in camouflaging minor stains.

4. Apron: Serving as a protective barrier, aprons shield the chef from hot spills and keep their uniform clean.

Footwear

1. Slip-Resistant Shoes: The kitchen can be a hazardous place with wet and slippery floors. Slip-resistant shoes are essential in preventing accidents.

2. Closed-Toe Design: This protects the feet from hot spills, dropped knives, and heavy objects.

Accessories

1. Gloves: As discussed in the previous section, gloves can prevent cross-contamination, especially when handling raw ingredients.

2. Thermometers and Timer: Worn around the neck or attached to the coat, these tools ensure food is cooked to the proper temperature and safe for consumption.

3. Hairnets and Beard Nets: These are vital in preventing hair from contaminating food. While the chef's hat serves this purpose to a degree, hairnets provide additional assurance, especially for those with long hair or beards.

Server's Attire

While servers may not be directly involved in food preparation, their attire is equally crucial in maintaining a clean environment and presenting a professional image.

1. **Uniforms:** These should be neat, clean, and well-fitting. Stained or unkempt uniforms can tarnish the establishment's image.

2. **Hair:** Should be tied back or neatly arranged to prevent it from coming into contact with food or plates.

3. **Minimal Jewelry:** Jewelry can be a potential source of contamination. It's advisable for servers to wear minimal jewelry, avoiding especially loose or dangly pieces.

4. **Name Tags and Badges:** These should be securely fastened and kept clean.

2.5 Managing Employee Illnesses and Injuries

When an employee in the food service industry falls ill or suffers an injury, there's an inherent risk of contaminating food, surfaces, and utensils. Common ailments like colds or the flu can be easily transmitted to food or to other workers, putting both staff and customers at risk. Moreover, open wounds or burns can lead to bacterial transmission if not properly covered and managed.

The key is to understand these risks, to recognize their potential consequences, and to be prepared to take immediate and appropriate action.

Every food establishment should have a well-defined illness policy that is communicated to all employees upon their induction and routinely thereafter. Such a policy should cover:

1. Reporting Procedures: Employees must know whom to inform if they're feeling unwell or suspect they have a contagious illness. Immediate reporting ensures swift action can be taken to minimize risks.

2. Exclusion from Work: There are certain illnesses, particularly gastrointestinal ones like norovirus or E. coli infections, where affected employees should be excluded from work. Establish a clear list of such illnesses and conditions under which employees can return.

3. Return-to-Work Protocols: Once an employee is recovering, there should be clear guidelines about when and how they can return to work. For instance, they might return to work but be restricted from handling food until they're completely symptom-free.

Addressing Injuries in the Workplace

Injuries, whether they're minor cuts or more severe burns, should be addressed with utmost care to prevent contamination and further harm.

1. First-Aid Kits: Every establishment should have easily accessible and well-stocked first-aid kits. Employees should be trained in basic first-aid procedures and know the location of these kits.

2. Reporting and Treatment: Any injury, no matter how minor, should be reported to a supervisor. If an injury is severe, seeking immediate medical attention is crucial.

3. Protective Measures: For minor wounds, using waterproof bandages and gloves can prevent contamination. In the case of burns, the affected area should be covered with a clean, non-stick bandage.

Education is the cornerstone of effective illness and injury management. Periodic training sessions can ensure that:

- Employees are aware of the potential risks associated with illnesses and injuries in the food service setting.
- Staff understand the importance of personal hygiene and self-monitoring.
- Workers can identify the symptoms of common foodborne illnesses.
- Everyone knows the protocols for reporting and managing health concerns.

2.6 Staff Training and Awareness

Within the food service environment, the potential for health hazards – from cross-contamination to the spread of foodborne illnesses – is ever-present. The diverse range of risks necessitates comprehensive training to ensure each staff member is not only aware of these hazards but also equipped to mitigate them.

1. Consistency: Regular training ensures that all staff members, regardless of their role, maintain consistent hygiene practices. This uniformity is critical to prevent lapses that might compromise food safety.

2. Compliance: Many regions have stringent regulations concerning food safety. Training ensures compliance with these standards, protecting businesses from potential legal repercussions and preserving their reputations.

3. Proactive Approach: Training transforms reactive practices into proactive ones. Rather than addressing issues after they arise, trained staff can prevent many of these problems from occurring in the first place.

Methods to Foster Training and Awareness

Achieving effective staff training and awareness doesn't hinge on a singular approach. Multiple methods, often used in tandem, can cater to diverse learning styles and ensure that every team member is well-informed and prepared.

1. Regular Workshops: Periodic workshops led by experts can provide hands-on training, allowing staff to learn and practice in real-time. These sessions can cover various topics, from hand-washing techniques to the safe handling of allergens.

2. Online Courses: In today's digital age, online courses offer flexibility. They can be accessed anytime, anywhere, and can be tailored to fit individual learning paces.

3. On-the-Job Training: New employees can benefit immensely from shadowing seasoned staff members. This method offers real-world insights and direct experiential learning.

4. Visual Aids: Posters, infographics, and videos can serve as constant reminders in the workplace. Positioned strategically, these aids can visually reinforce crucial hygiene practices.

Creating a Culture of Awareness

While training sessions and courses are vital, fostering an ongoing culture of awareness is equally significant. This involves:

1. **Open Communication:** Encouraging staff to voice concerns, ask questions, and share insights can foster a collaborative environment where everyone learns from one another.

2. **Regular Updates:** As the world of food safety evolves, so should training methods. Keeping staff updated with the latest best practices and industry standards is key.

3. **Recognition:** Recognizing and rewarding employees who consistently demonstrate exemplary hygiene practices can motivate others to follow suit.

An often overlooked, yet invaluable method of enhancing training is soliciting feedback. Post-training surveys or open forums where employees can discuss what they found beneficial or suggest areas for improvement can greatly inform future training sessions.

Chapter 3: Purchasing, Receiving, and Storage

3.1 Supplier Selection

The safety and quality of the food served in an establishment are largely dependent on the initial selection of suppliers. With the increasing complexity of the global food supply chain, ensuring that your suppliers adhere to best practices is not only beneficial for the bottom line but also vital for public health.

Suppliers are the initial point of entry for the products that an establishment will process, cook, and serve. The quality of these products significantly influences the final product's safety and integrity. Therefore, making informed decisions during the supplier selection process is not just a procurement strategy but a foundational aspect of food safety.

Criteria for Supplier Selection

Several factors come into play when selecting a supplier. Here are the primary criteria:

1. **Compliance with Regulations:** Ensure that the supplier consistently meets local, state, and national food safety standards and regulations. Certifications and licenses can serve as proof of such compliance.

2. **Track Record of Quality:** Investigate the supplier's history concerning product recalls, reported contaminations, or any other red flags that could indicate lapses in quality control.

3. **Capability for Traceability:** It's vital for a supplier to track products back to their origins. Such traceability can be instrumental if a recall becomes necessary or if the source of contamination needs to be identified.

4. Financial Stability: A supplier in good financial health is often more likely to have consistent operations and less likely to compromise on quality to save costs.

5. Responsiveness and Communication: Establishing a clear communication channel with the supplier ensures timely resolution of concerns and can be vital when addressing urgent quality or safety issues.

6. References and Reviews: Look for references or reviews from other businesses that have partnered with the supplier. These can offer insights into the supplier's reliability and consistency.

Evaluation Techniques

Once you've outlined your criteria, the next step is the actual evaluation. Here's a structured approach:

1. Request for Information (RFI): Begin with an RFI to gather basic data about the supplier's capabilities, certifications, and operational details.

2. On-Site Audits: Conducting physical audits of the supplier's facilities provides firsthand insights into their operations, hygiene practices, and overall commitment to quality.

3. Product Sampling: Procure samples of the products you intend to purchase and conduct independent quality and safety tests.

4. Negotiation and Agreement: Once satisfied, enter into detailed negotiations to agree on terms, prices, and quality benchmarks. Ensure all safety and quality expectations are explicitly mentioned in the contractual agreement.

Supplier evaluation is not a one-and-done process. Continuous monitoring and periodic reviews are necessary to ensure that the supplier remains compliant and upholds the agreed-upon standards.

3.2 Receiving Procedures

When food shipments arrive at your establishment, they're transitioning from a controlled environment maintained by the supplier to your own controlled environment. This transition is a critical moment. If compromised products are accepted, they could contaminate other goods, endangering the health of consumers and potentially leading to significant financial and reputational repercussions for the business.

Checking Temperatures Upon Arrival

Ensuring that food items are received at the correct temperature is vital to prevent the growth of harmful pathogens.

- **Cold Foods**: Cold foods, such as meats, dairy, and certain produce, should be received at a temperature of 41°F (5°C) or below, unless specified otherwise by regulations or the product's nature.
- **Frozen Foods**: Frozen products should be solid with no visible signs of thawing.
- **Hot Foods**: Items meant to be received hot, like soups or pre-prepared meals, should maintain a temperature of 135°F (57°C) or higher.

Using infrared or probe thermometers is recommended for quick and accurate readings. Regular calibration of these devices ensures accuracy.

Checking Conditions of Food Shipments

1. **Packaging**: Ensure that packaging is intact and undamaged. Torn or compromised packages can be a sign of contamination or pest activity.

2. **Expiration Dates**: All products should be checked for their use-by or expiration dates. Products nearing their expiration should be flagged, and those past their date should be rejected.

3. **Signs of Contamination**: Look for signs of mold, off-odors, or any other evidence that indicates spoilage.

4. **Dry Goods:** Items like grains, cereals, and pasta should be free from moisture, which can promote microbial growth.

5. **Documentation**: Always ensure that the received shipment comes with the necessary documentation, detailing product information, source, and any other pertinent data.

Organizing the Receiving Area

- Maintaining a systematic and clean receiving area plays a crucial role in the efficient inspection of incoming goods.
- Designate specific areas for inspection, ensuring adequate lighting and necessary tools at hand.
- Maintain a schedule for deliveries to avoid congestion and allow adequate time for thorough checks.
- Employ trained personnel for receiving tasks. Their training should emphasize the importance of this step and provide them with the skills to detect inconsistencies.

Handling Rejections

Not all shipments will meet your established standards. In cases where products do not meet criteria:

- Isolate rejected items from the accepted ones.
- Clearly mark the rejected products and inform the supplier immedi-

ately.

- Maintain a log of rejections, detailing the reason for rejection, the supplier, date, and any other relevant details. This data can be valuable for future supplier evaluations.

3.3 Proper Storage: the FIFO System

Proper food storage plays a pivotal role in:

- Maximizing Shelf Life: Proper storage conditions can help preserve the freshness and quality of food items, reducing waste and increasing profitability.
- Preventing Cross-contamination: Organizing and segregating food items can prevent the spread of bacteria or allergens.
- Ensuring Food Safety: Storing foods at their required temperatures can inhibit the growth of harmful pathogens, protecting consumer health.

Storage Sequence: The FIFO Method

One of the foundational principles of food storage is the First-In, First-Out (FIFO) method:

Understanding FIFO: This principle ensures that older inventory is used before newer inventory. As new shipments arrive, they're placed behind the older products. This rotation ensures that items don't expire or degrade in quality before they're used.

Implementing FIFO: Clearly label all items with their receiving date. Training staff to always check these dates before using products can ensure adherence to the FIFO principle.

Temperature Zones: Cold and Dry Storage

Temperature plays a pivotal role in food storage. Different products have different temperature requirements, and meeting these requirements can prevent spoilage and ensure safety.

Cold Storage: Refrigerators should maintain temperatures at or below 40°F (4°C), while freezers should be at 0°F (-18°C) or lower. Regularly monitoring these temperatures with calibrated thermometers is vital.

Refrigerated Storage: Items like dairy, meat, poultry, and seafood require cold storage. Produce, like fruits and vegetables, may also require refrigeration, depending on their type and ripeness.

Frozen Storage: Foods meant to be stored frozen should remain solid with no signs of freezer burn or thawing.

Dry Storage: This is for items that don't require refrigeration. The storage area should be cool, dry, and well-ventilated, ideally between 50°F (10°C) and 70°F (21°C). Humidity levels should be kept below 60% to prevent mold growth.

Organizing the Storage Area

The way items are organized within the storage area can affect both their quality and safety.

Separation by Type: Meat, poultry, seafood, dairy, and produce should all have designated areas within cold storage. This segregation can prevent cross-contamination.

Vertical Organization: In refrigerated storage, raw meats should be stored on the lowest shelves to prevent their juices from contaminating other foods. Ready-to-eat or cooked foods should be stored on higher shelves.

Air Circulation: Ensure there's enough space between items and that storage areas aren't overcrowded. Adequate air circulation can be useful in maintaining stable temperatures.

Clear Labeling: Every item should be clearly labeled with its name, receiving date, and expiration date if applicable.

3.4 Inventory Management

Effective inventory management can prevent contamination, reduce waste, and ultimately ensure the delivery of fresh and safe food to customers.

The Dual Role of Inventory Management

- Economic Impact: Inventory management directly affects the bottom line. Efficient management reduces waste, avoids unnecessary purchases, and ensures resources are used optimally.
- Safety Impact: Proper storage and rotation practices, integral components of inventory management, prevent food contamination, thus ensuring consumer safety.

Strategies for Preventing Contamination

1. **Separation of Foods:**

Raw and cooked foods should be stored separately to prevent cross-contamination.

Raw meats, poultry, and seafood should be stored in containers or trays at the bottom shelves of refrigerators to prevent drippings from contaminating other foods.

2. **Sealed Containers:**

Foods, especially those in a raw state or those that are particularly vulnerable to contamination, should be stored in well-sealed containers.

Transparent containers can be advantageous as they allow for visual inspections without the need to open them, reducing exposure.

3. **Regular Cleaning:**

Storage areas, including refrigerators, freezers, and dry storage, should be cleaned regularly. This not only ensures a sanitary environment but also prevents pests.

4. **Controlled Access:**

Limit access to storage areas to trained staff only. This reduces the chances of contamination through unnecessary handling or exposure.

Strategies for Preventing Waste

1. Adhere to FIFO:

   As discussed in the previous section, the First In, First Out (FIFO) system ensures that older inventory is used first, reducing the chances of spoilage.

2. Regular Inventory Checks:

   Routine inventory checks can help identify items nearing their expiration date, allowing for timely usage or reordering as necessary.

3. Monitoring Storage Conditions:

   Regularly monitor and adjust storage conditions, such as temperature and humidity, to ensure they are optimal for the stored items.

4. Purchase Planning:

   Base purchasing decisions on actual consumption data and avoid over-ordering. While bulk purchases can offer cost savings, they can lead to waste if products aren't consumed before they deteriorate.

5. Use of Technology

Digital Inventory Systems: These systems can track products in real-time, send alerts for products nearing expiration, and provide consumption analytics to aid in purchasing decisions.

6. Temperature Monitoring Devices: Devices equipped with alarms can alert staff if storage temperatures deviate from the optimal range, ensuring timely intervention.

Staff Training and Engagement

Continuous Training: Regular training sessions can ensure that staff are updated on best practices, new technologies, and the importance of their role in inventory management.

Incentives for Reduction of Waste: Some establishments offer incentives to teams or individuals that suggest or implement strategies leading to noticeable reductions in waste.

Chapter 4: Preparation, Cooking and Serving

4.1 Safe Food Preparation

The act of **cleaning food products**, particularly fresh produce, serves as the first line of defense against potential contaminants. Soil, pesticides, bacteria, and even insects can linger on the surfaces of fruits and vegetables.

1. Water is Paramount:

   Every piece of fresh produce should be washed under cold running water before preparation. Refrain from using soaps or other chemicals unless they're food-safe and specifically designed for this purpose.

2. Special Care for Specific Produce:

   Leafy greens or vegetables with crevices, like broccoli, can harbor more dirt and microbes. These items may benefit from a brief soak in cold water before being rinsed.

3. Cleaning Non-produce Items:

   Eggs, for instance, should never be washed as it can remove their protective outer layer. However, their shells should be cleaned with a cloth or brush before breaking.

Cutting

When it comes to cutting, precision is crucial, not just for the culinary presentation but also for safety.

Separate Boards and Knives:

Always use separate cutting boards and knives for raw and cooked foods.

This prevents cross-contamination. For instance, a knife that has cut raw chicken should never be used to chop vegetables for a salad unless it has been thoroughly washed.

Regular Maintenance:

Keeping knives sharp is paradoxically one of the best ways to prevent accidents. A sharp knife is less likely to slip while cutting.

Safe Practices:

Techniques such as the 'claw grip' can help prevent accidental cuts. Always cut away from the body and keep fingers clear of the blade's path.

Marinating

Marinating not only imparts depth and flavor to foods but can also tenderize certain meats. However, this process, if done incorrectly, can become a source of foodborne illnesses.

Always Marinate in the Refrigerator

Marinating at room temperature can allow harmful bacteria to proliferate. Always ensure that marinating foods are kept in the refrigerator.

Use Non-reactive Containers

Acids in marinades can react with certain metals. Glass or food-safe plastic containers are preferred for marinating.

Avoid Cross-contamination

Never reuse marinade from raw meat or poultry unless it's boiled first to destroy any harmful bacteria.

Timing is Crucial

While some foods benefit from long marination times, others can become over-marinated, leading to a mushy texture. Adhere to recommended marinating times for the best results.

4.2 Cooking Techniques and Internal Temperatures

At its core, the reason we emphasize internal temperatures lies in the battle against pathogenic bacteria. These harmful microbes can cause foodborne illnesses when ingested. Cooking food to the right internal temperature ensures the destruction of these pathogens.

However, it's not just about hitting a high temperature. The amount of time the food stays at that temperature, known as the "thermal death time," also plays a crucial role. For instance, some bacteria might survive a brief moment at a high temperature but will be eradicated if that temperature is maintained for a longer period.

Common Cooking Techniques and Their Temperature Dynamics

- **Roasting and Baking:** Used primarily for meats, poultry, and baked goods. The slow, consistent heat of an oven ensures even cooking. For meats, a thermometer inserted into the thickest part away from bone should register the recommended temperature for that specific meat type. For instance, poultry should be cooked to an internal temperature of 165°F (74°C) to ensure safety.

- **Grilling and Broiling:** These high-heat methods are popular for their ability to impart a charred flavor. Yet, they can be tricky in ensuring even cooking, especially with thicker cuts. Regularly flipping and monitoring the internal temperature is crucial. Steaks, for example, have varying levels of "doneness," but for safety, a medium-rare steak should have an internal temperature of at least 145°F (63°C).

- **Boiling and Simmering**: Often used for vegetables, pastas, and soups. While boiling is a high-heat method, simmering is its gentler cousin. When cooking meats in soups or stews, the broth's temperature can be an indicator, but always verify the meat's internal temperature.

- **Sautéing and Pan-frying**: These are quick-cooking methods, often used for vegetables and thinner meat cuts. As the food is cooked quickly over high heat, it's essential to cut foods in uniform sizes to ensure even cooking. Despite the rapid cook time, the internal temperatures for safety still apply.

- **Steaming:** Renowned for preserving the nutritional content of vegetables. When steaming foods like fish or dumplings, ensure that they are evenly spaced and in a single layer to guarantee consistent cooking. For fish, the flesh should flake easily with a fork when adequately cooked.

After cooking, it's advisable to let meats "rest." This isn't just a culinary trick to ensure juiciness. As meat rests, its residual heat continues to cook it slightly, potentially raising the internal temperature a few more degrees. This can be a final safeguard in ensuring that the meat has reached a safe temperature throughout.

4.3 Holding Food Safely

After cooking, an equally crucial phase of food service is the holding stage. This process, seemingly simple, carries a profound weight in ensuring food safety. It is imperative to maintain specific temperature ranges when holding food, whether hot or cold. Overlooking this can lead to the proliferation of harmful bacteria, jeopardizing public health and an establishment's reputation.

The Danger Zone: Understanding its Significance

Central to the discussion of food holding is the concept of the "Danger Zone" - the temperature range in which bacteria can grow most rapidly. This zone spans from 41°F (5°C) to 135°F (57°C). When food sits within this range for prolonged periods, it becomes vulnerable to bacterial growth. Therefore, the chief aim of proper food holding is to keep food outside this temperature bracket, ensuring its safety for consumption.

Hot Holding Guidelines

The essence of hot holding is maintaining cooked food's temperature at or above the designated safe temperature, which is generally recognized as 135°F (57°C). Here's how to accomplish this effectively:

1. **Use Appropriate Equipment**: Employ devices specifically designed for hot holding, such as steam tables, heat lamps, and hot holding cabinets. These devices should consistently hold food at the correct temperature, without the need for frequent adjustments.

2. **Regular Temperature Checks**: Even with the best equipment, regularly monitoring the temperature of the food is vital. Use calibrated thermometers to check the temperature at least every two hours. Remember, the goal is to catch any potential drop in temperature before it reaches the danger zone.

3. **Stirring**: Foods held in large containers, like soups or sauces, benefit from occasional stirring. This practice ensures even heat distribution throughout the dish.

4. **Covering the Food**: Keeping the food covered minimizes its exposure to potential contaminants and aids in maintaining consistent temperatures. Use lids or aluminum foils, ensuring they're removed using clean and sanitized utensils or gloves.

Cold Holding Guidelines

For cold holding, the aim is the inverse of hot holding: keeping food at or below 41°F (5°C). Here's how:

1. **Refrigeration**: A straightforward method, but ensuring that the refrigerator operates efficiently and is not overloaded is paramount. An overstuffed refrigerator can lead to inconsistent cooling.

2. **Ice Baths:** For some foods, especially those served in buffet settings, using ice baths can be practical. Ensure the ice surrounds the food container and reaches a level higher than the food itself. As with hot foods, regular temperature checks are vital.

3. **Time as a Control Mechanism**: Sometimes, establishments use time, rather than temperature, to ensure food safety. In such cases, food should not be left out for more than six hours and should be discarded if its temperature exceeds 70°F (21°C) during that period.

4. **Rapid Cooling Techniques:** When transitioning hot foods to cold storage, rapid cooling techniques can be employed. Methods include dividing the food into smaller portions, using ice paddles, or utilizing blast chillers.

During the holding phase, whether hot or cold, always be vigilant about preventing cross-contamination. Use separate utensils for different foods and ensure that raw foods, especially meats, are held separately from cooked or ready-to-eat foods.

4.4 Serving and Presentation

Cross-contamination occurs when harmful microorganisms or allergens transfer from one surface, food, or individual to another, presenting health risks. This transfer can happen through direct contact or indirectly, via equipment, utensils, or even the air. For establishments that pride themselves on their culinary creations, an incident of cross-contamination can tarnish their reputation, leading to decreased trust and potential legal ramifications.

Several facets of serving and presentation harbor the risk of cross-contamination. These include:

1. **Utensils and Equipment**: The tools used for serving must be strictly dedicated to that purpose. For instance, a knife used to cut raw poultry should never be used to slice fruits without a thorough wash in between.

2. **Server Hygiene:** The staff responsible for serving must adhere to impeccable personal hygiene standards. Hands should be washed frequently, especially after handling raw foods, money, or attending to personal needs.

3. **Plating Area:** The area where food is plated should be clean and sanitized, away from raw food preparation zones. Any spills should be immediately addressed to prevent the potential spread of pathogens.

4. **Food Garnishes:** Often overlooked, garnishes can be a source of cross-contamination. Ensure they are stored properly, and hands or utensils used for garnishing are clean.

Preventative Measures

To mitigate the risks associated with serving and presentation, consider the following guidelines:

1. **Dedicated Utensils and Equipment:** Assign specific tools for specific tasks. Color-coding can be an effective method. For instance,

red-handled knives for meats and green for vegetables can instantly signal their intended purpose to staff.

2. **Regular Training**: All staff, not just those in food preparation, should undergo regular training sessions on food safety, emphasizing the importance of avoiding cross-contamination.

3. **Proper Storage**: Store ready-to-serve or cooked foods separately from raw ones, even in the serving area. For instance, salads ready for serving should not share shelf space with raw proteins.

4. **Monitor Temperature**: Just as with holding, ensure that foods meant to be served cold are kept adequately chilled until they reach the table. Similarly, hot dishes should remain hot, minimizing the time they spend in the danger zone of temperature.

5. **Allergen Awareness**: With the rise in food allergies, it's paramount to ensure dishes meant to be allergen-free are not cross-contaminated with potential allergens. This might mean having separate serving tools or even areas for allergen-free dishes.

While safety is paramount, the aesthetics of a dish contribute significantly to the dining experience. Hence, as establishments focus on preventing cross-contamination, equal emphasis should be placed on the visual appeal of the dish. The colors, arrangement, and even the choice of plate can enhance a diner's experience.

However, remember that garnishes and additions to the plate should always be edible and fresh. Avoid using stale or sub-par ingredients purely for visual appeal, as this compromises the overall integrity and safety of the dish.

4.5 Equipment and Utensil Usage

The kitchen, often considered the heart of a culinary establishment, is replete with tools designed for specific tasks. From knives that dice to blenders that purée, each utensil and piece of equipment has a defined role. Their correct usage ensures efficiency, consistency, and safety. However, mismanagement can result in cross-contamination, uneven cooking, and even injuries.

Common Mistakes in Equipment and Utensil Usage

1. **Cross-Contamination via Utensils**: One of the most frequent mistakes is using the same utensil for different food items without proper cleaning in between. For instance, using a knife that just diced raw chicken to slice tomatoes can introduce harmful pathogens to the vegetable.

2. **Overloading Equipment**: Many make the mistake of overfilling machines like food processors or blenders. This not only reduces the efficiency of the equipment but can also lead to uneven preparation and increased wear and tear.

3. **Ignoring Manufacturer Guidelines**: Every piece of equipment comes with a user manual that provides guidelines on its operation, cleaning, and maintenance. Overlooking these instructions can lead to mishaps and reduced equipment longevity.

4. **Using Damaged Equipment:** Continuing to use chipped, broken, or malfunctioning equipment is a safety hazard. For instance, using a cracked mixing bowl can introduce fragments into the food.

How to Avoid These Mistakes

1. Dedicated Utensils for Different Tasks: Assign specific utensils for distinct functions. For instance, have separate cutting boards and knives for raw meats, vegetables, and ready-to-eat foods. This division reduces the risk

of cross-contamination.

2. Regular Equipment Inspection: Schedule routine checks of all kitchen equipment. Look for signs of wear and tear, damage, or malfunction. Address any issues immediately, either by repairing or replacing the equipment.

3. Adhere to Manufacturer Guidelines: Always refer to the user manual when operating, cleaning, or maintaining any equipment. These guidelines are there to ensure the equipment's efficient and safe operation.

4. Proper Training: Ensure that all kitchen staff are adequately trained in the use of all equipment and utensils. Regular training sessions can update them on best practices and safety protocols.

5. Clean and Sanitize: After every use, clean and sanitize equipment and utensils thoroughly. Not only does this practice prevent cross-contamination, but it also ensures the longevity of the tools.

6. Avoid Overloading: Be mindful of the capacity limits of equipment. Overfilling can result in spills, uneven processing, and increased strain on the machinery.

A chef's skill is undeniably paramount in culinary arts. However, even the most skilled chef requires tools that are in prime condition and are used correctly. The relationship between a chef and their tools is symbiotic. The chef's prowess can elevate a dish, but the right tool, used correctly, ensures consistency, efficiency, and safety.

Chapter 5: Facilities, Cleaning/Sanitizing, and Pest Management

5.1 Facility Requirements

Facilities play a paramount role in the journey of food, from raw ingredients to a finished dish. A well-designed and maintained facility ensures that food is prepared, cooked, and stored in optimal conditions, preventing contamination and ensuring the highest quality. Conversely, a lackluster facility can become a breeding ground for pathogens, cross-contamination, and inefficiencies.

Key Components of an Effective Food Prep Space

1. **Layout and Design:** The food prep space must be logically designed to allow for an efficient workflow. The flow should minimize cross-movement and potential contamination. For instance, raw ingredients should have a clear path from receiving to storage to preparation without crossing paths with ready-to-eat foods.

2. **Material and Surfaces:** All surfaces, from countertops to floors, must be made of non-porous, easy-to-clean materials. Stainless steel is often preferred for countertops because of its resistance to microbial growth and its durability. Floors should be slip-resistant and capable of withstanding frequent cleaning.

3. **Ventilation**: Proper ventilation ensures a steady flow of fresh air, minimizing condensation and preventing the buildup of harmful fumes or bacteria. Hood systems above cooking areas are essential to capture steam, smoke, and particulates.

4. **Lighting:** Good lighting is not just about visibility; it also plays a role in staff morale and safety. Shadows can cause accidents, especially around knives and hot surfaces. Moreover, adequate lighting can aid in

spotting contaminants or spoilage.

5. **Temperature Control:** The facility should be equipped with proper heating, ventilation, and air conditioning (HVAC) systems to ensure temperature consistency. This is crucial not only for the comfort of the staff but also to maintain the integrity of certain foods.

6. **Waste Management:** Disposal areas should be strategically located to ensure waste doesn't cross-contaminate food areas. Additionally, they should be easy to clean and, where necessary, refrigerated to prevent the growth of bacteria.

7. **Handwashing Stations:** An often-overlooked yet critical component, handwashing stations should be easily accessible. They need to be stocked with soap, hot water, and disposable towels, encouraging staff to practice regular hand hygiene.

8. **Storage Areas:** These areas, both dry and cold, should be spacious, well-organized, and designed to prevent cross-contamination. Shelving should be off the ground, and foods should be stored in a manner that prevents drips or spills onto other foods.

Regular maintenance checks and proactive measures are vital in keeping a food prep facility in optimal condition. This includes routine inspections for wear and tear, ensuring equipment is functioning efficiently, and addressing any potential issues before they escalate. A commitment to cleanliness is paramount, with regular deep cleaning schedules to ensure every nook and cranny of the facility is sanitized.

5.2 Daily Cleaning and Sanitizing Procedures

Before delving into the procedures, it's essential to distinguish between cleaning and sanitizing. Cleaning refers to the removal of visible dirt, grime, and impurities from surfaces. It's the act of physically scrubbing and washing to rid an area or item of debris. Sanitizing, on the other hand, concerns the reduction of pathogens and microorganisms on cleaned surfaces to safe levels. While cleaning removes visible dirt, sanitizing ensures that the invisible harmful bacteria are minimized.

Both processes are crucial and complementary. A surface cannot be properly sanitized if it has not been cleaned first.

Routine Daily Cleaning Tasks

Every culinary establishment, irrespective of its size, must prioritize certain cleaning tasks each day:

1. **Floors**: Begin with sweeping to remove larger debris. Mopping should follow, using appropriate floor cleaners. Special attention must be given to areas that are prone to spills or grease buildup, like around fryers or grills.

2. **Countertops and Preparation Areas:** These areas are the heart of the kitchen and see a lot of activity. After each use, they should be wiped down with warm soapy water and then sanitized.

3. **Equipment and Utensils:** After each use, equipment and tools, such as knives, pots, and pans, should be washed in hot soapy water, rinsed, and then sanitized. Larger equipment like ovens and grills might require specialized cleaning agents and procedures.

4. **Sinks and Handwashing Stations**: Given their frequent use and their role in maintaining hygiene, sinks should be cleaned and sanitized multiple times throughout the day.

5. **Waste Disposal Areas**: Trash bins should be emptied regularly, and the containers themselves should be cleaned and sanitized daily to pre-

vent bacterial growth and odors.

6. **Storage Areas**: While they might not require intensive daily cleaning, it's good practice to check them for any spills or signs of pest activity.

Routine Daily Sanitizing Methods

After cleaning, sanitizing ensures the reduction of harmful pathogens. Here are some general methods:

1. **Heat Sanitizing:** This involves immersing items in hot water at temperatures often above 171°F (77°C). This method is common for utensils and dishes.

2. **Chemical Sanitizing**: This method employs chemical solutions, like chlorine-based or quaternary ammonium-based sanitizers. It's essential to follow manufacturer instructions to ensure the effective reduction of pathogens without leaving harmful residues.

3. **Surface Sanitizing**: For larger surfaces that cannot be immersed in solutions or subjected to high heat, sanitizing sprays or wipes can be used. Again, allowing the sanitizer to sit for the recommended contact time is crucial for its efficacy.

Ensuring Effectiveness and Safety

To maintain the integrity of cleaning and sanitizing procedures:

1. **Regularly Train Staff:** All kitchen staff should be well-versed in cleaning and sanitizing procedures. Regular training ensures that everyone is updated on best practices.

2. **Use the Right Concentrations:** Especially with chemical sanitizers, it's imperative to use the correct concentration. Too little might be ineffective, while too much could be unsafe.

3. **Frequently Change Cleaning Solutions**: Dirty water or solutions won't clean effectively. Ensure that cleaning solutions are changed regularly.

4. **Check Equipment and Tools**: Regularly inspect equipment and tools for signs of wear and tear. Damaged equipment can harbor bacteria and might not be cleaned effectively.

5.3 Recommended Cleaning Products and Tools

Every cleaning task in a kitchen or food prep area has its unique challenges. The grease that accumulates on a grill is distinct from the mineral buildup in a dishwasher, and thus, each requires specialized cleaning agents and tools for effective removal. Employing the correct products not only ensures cleanliness but also extends the lifespan of kitchen equipment and tools.

General Cleaners

For areas with less grease or baked-on food, a general-purpose cleaner is sufficient. These are typically pH neutral and are safe for most surfaces. They're ideal for:

- Daily cleaning of floors and walls.
- Cleaning countertops and tables after wiping away food residues.
- External cleaning of appliances like refrigerators or ovens.

Degreasers

Kitchens see a lot of grease, especially around frying areas. A degreaser is designed to break down oils and fats, making them easier to wipe or rinse away. Key applications include:

- Cleaning grills, fryers, and ovens.
- Removing grease spills on floors.
- Cleaning exhaust hoods and fans.

Descalers

Water with high mineral content can leave deposits on equipment and surfaces. Descalers or delimers dissolve these mineral deposits. They are crucial for:

- Coffee makers, where mineral buildup can affect the taste of beverages.
- Dishwashers, ensuring they function efficiently.
- Faucets and sinks to maintain a clean appearance.

Sanitizers

While cleaning removes visible dirt, sanitizers reduce pathogens to safe levels. Two primary types of sanitizers are used in kitchens:

1. **Heat:** Often used for dishwashing, where utensils and dishes are exposed to high temperatures.
2. **Chemical:** Solutions like chlorine or quaternary ammonium compounds. These are used on countertops, cutting boards, and other surfaces after cleaning.

Essential Tools for Cleaning

Brushes

A variety of brushes, each designed for specific tasks, aids in the cleaning process. For instance:

- **Grill brushes** with stiff bristles are perfect for scrubbing away charred food residues.
- **Bottle brushes** with elongated handles assist in cleaning narrow vessels or tubes in equipment.
- **Detail brushes** are vital for reaching nooks and crannies in equipment or intricate tools.

Cloths and Sponges

Reusable or disposable, these are essential for wiping surfaces:

- Microfiber cloths are excellent for general cleaning due to their ability to trap dirt and dust.
- Cellulose sponges are absorbent and are great for wiping down large surfaces or cleaning up spills.

Scrub Pads

These are vital for tasks that need a bit more abrasion:

- Stainless steel or copper scrub pads are ideal for heavy-duty cleaning tasks like pots with burnt food.
- Non-scratch scrub pads are suited for delicate surfaces like glass or

non-stick pans.

Mops and Buckets

For floor cleaning:

- Wet mops are used with cleaning solutions to clean the floor.
- Dry mops or dust mops help in collecting dust and loose debris.

Considerations When Choosing Products and Tools

1. Material Compatibility: Ensure that the cleaning product or tool is safe for the material it's being used on.
2. Environmental Impact: Eco-friendly products can effectively clean and have a lesser environmental footprint.
3. Frequency of Use: If an area or tool is cleaned frequently, choose products that are gentle yet effective.
4. Storage: Cleaning products should be stored safely, away from food prep areas, and out of reach of unauthorized personnel or children.

5.4 Pest Identification and Prevention

Pests in the food service industry pose a significant threat, not only to the reputation of the establishment but, more importantly, to the health of its customers and the integrity of its products. The presence of pests can lead to contamination, disease transmission, and regulatory penalties. Identifying common pests, understanding their habits, and implementing prevention strategies are crucial to maintaining a hygienic and safe environment.

Common Pests in the Food Service Industry

Rodents (Rats and Mice):

Rodents are a perennial problem in many establishments due to their ability to find food and shelter. Their droppings, hair, and urine can contaminate food, surfaces, and utensils, leading to a host of diseases, including salmonellosis and hantavirus. Rats and mice are also known to cause structural damage by gnawing on wires, pipes, and other infrastructure.

Cockroaches:

These nocturnal creatures can survive in a variety of environments, making them particularly challenging to eliminate. They carry a range of pathogens on their bodies and in their feces, which can cause diseases like dysentery, gastroenteritis, and typhoid.

Flies:

Flies, especially houseflies and fruit flies, are notorious for their ability to spread diseases. They can transmit harmful microorganisms from decaying matter and waste to food and surfaces.

Stored Product Insects (SPIs):

These pests infest dry food products like grains, cereals, dried fruits, and nuts. Common SPIs include weevils, beetles, and moths.

Ants:

While generally less hazardous than other pests, ants can be a nuisance in food service areas. They can contaminate food as they forage and compromise the cleanliness of the environment.

Understanding Pest Behavior and Habitats

Understanding the behavior of these pests can assist in identifying infestations early and addressing them efficiently. For instance:

- Rodents are known to leave grease marks along walls and can be detected by their droppings or gnaw marks.
- Cockroaches prefer dark, moist environments like cracks, crevices, or under kitchen equipment.
- Flies are attracted to decaying organic matter and moist environments.
- SPIs usually infest food products that have been stored for prolonged periods without disturbance.

Prevention Strategies

1. **Regular Inspections:** Routinely inspect your facility, paying special attention to potential entry points, storage areas, and food preparation zones. Look for signs of pests, such as droppings, gnaw marks, or damaged food packaging.

2. **Sanitation:** Cleanliness is the first line of defense against pests. Ensure that food residues are promptly cleaned up, trash is regularly taken out, and spills are addressed immediately.

3. **Proper Storage:** Store food in sealed, pest-proof containers. Elevate stored items off the ground to deter pests like rodents.

4. **Seal Entry Points:** Pests can enter through the smallest of openings. Ensure that windows and doors have tight-fitting screens. Seal cracks, crevices, and any openings with caulk or other appropriate materials.

5. **Professional Pest Control**: Establish a relationship with a licensed pest control service. Regular treatments can prevent infestations and address any emerging issues promptly.

6. **Employee Training:** Ensure that all staff are trained to recognize

the signs of pest infestations and understand the importance of preventative measures.

5.5 Infestation Action Plans

The detection of pests in a food service environment can be alarming, given the threats they pose to public health, food integrity, and the reputation of the establishment. Immediate and comprehensive action is necessary to manage and ultimately eradicate the infestation. An effective infestation action plan can make the difference between a swiftly resolved issue and an escalating problem. In this section, we will elucidate the steps an establishment should undertake if pests are detected, ensuring the safety and well-being of customers and staff.

1. Immediate Isolation:

When an infestation is identified, the immediate concern is containment. If the pest is discovered in a specific product, for instance, that product should be isolated to prevent cross-contamination. Similarly, if a certain area is found to be infested, access to that area should be restricted until remediation can occur.

2. Inform Management and Staff:

Swift communication is vital. Management should be notified of the situation immediately to ensure appropriate resources are allocated to address the issue. Additionally, staff should be informed so that they can be extra vigilant and assist in the containment and eradication processes.

3. Document the Infestation:

Documentation serves multiple purposes. Firstly, it offers a clear picture of the situation's severity, helping to guide intervention strategies. Secondly, it provides a record that can be useful for regulatory or insurance purposes. Details that should be documented include the type of pest, the extent of the infestation, affected areas or products, and any immediate actions taken.

4. Consult a Pest Control Professional:

While minor infestations might be manageable with in-house resources, a professional pest control company's expertise is usually required for significant issues. They can provide an assessment of the situation, recommend treatments, and guide the establishment through the eradication process.

5. Implement Treatment Protocols:

Based on the recommendations of the pest control professional, appropriate treatments should be implemented. This might include the application of pesticides, bait stations, or traps. It's crucial that any treatments are conducted safely, adhering to guidelines and ensuring no contamination of food or food-preparation areas.

6. Intensify Cleaning and Sanitation Efforts:

Pests are often attracted to food residues and waste. As part of the action plan, there should be a ramping up of cleaning and sanitation efforts. This means ensuring that food is stored correctly, waste is disposed of promptly, and any potential food sources for pests are eliminated.

7. Monitor the Situation:

After treatment, it's essential to closely monitor the situation to ensure the infestation is indeed under control. This involves regular inspections, tracking any signs of pests, and working with the pest control company to ensure that the problem is being effectively managed.

8. Evaluate and Revise Preventative Measures:

Once the immediate threat has been addressed, it's crucial to evaluate what went wrong and how a similar situation can be prevented in the future. This might involve revising storage protocols, sealing potential entry points, or establishing more frequent pest control visits.

9. Train Staff:

Employees play a pivotal role in both detecting and preventing infestations. Post-infestation, it's beneficial to conduct training sessions to educate staff about what went wrong and how they can be proactive in the future. This could include identifying signs of pests, understanding the importance of sanitation, and ensuring that food is stored correctly.

10. Communicate with Stakeholders:

While it might be tempting to keep an infestation quiet, transparency is crucial, especially if the public becomes aware of the issue. This means communicating with customers, suppliers, and regulators, if necessary, about the steps being taken to address the problem and ensure food safety.

5.6 Regular Facility Maintenance

At the heart of any successful food service establishment is a commitment to regular facility maintenance. This ongoing process, often underestimated, is crucial for several reasons:

- Safety Assurance: Properly maintained facilities are less likely to present safety hazards, such as electrical issues or structural problems.
- Regulatory Compliance: Health and safety regulations often man-

date certain maintenance routines, and failure to adhere can result in penalties or closure.

- Operational Efficiency: Regularly serviced equipment operates more efficiently, reducing energy costs and preventing unexpected breakdowns.

Routine Maintenance Checks

To uphold the standards expected in the food service industry, several routine checks should be part of the facility's maintenance schedule:

1. **Structural Integrity:** Periodically inspect the building's overall structure, including walls, floors, ceilings, and roofs. Look for signs of wear, damage, or potential entry points for pests.

2. **Plumbing Systems**: Regularly check faucets, sinks, and drains to ensure they are functioning correctly. Slow or clogged drains can become breeding grounds for pests and bacteria.

3. **Electrical Systems:** Ensure all electrical systems, including lights, outlets, and major appliances, are functioning correctly. Electrical malfunctions can pose a fire risk and disrupt operations.

4. **Ventilation and HVAC Systems:** Clean and service ventilation systems to ensure efficient airflow and temperature regulation. This aids in preventing mold growth and ensures a comfortable environment for staff and patrons.

5. **Equipment Operation:** Check the functionality of all kitchen appliances. Calibrate thermostats, and ensure that refrigeration units maintain appropriate temperatures.

6. **Fire Safety Systems:** Regularly inspect fire alarms, extinguishers, and suppression systems to ensure they are in operational condition.

7. **Waste Management:** Ensure waste disposal areas are clean and that waste is being disposed of correctly. This will help deter pests and reduce odors.

Chapter 6: Regulatory Authorities

6.1 Overview of Major Regulatory Bodies

In the vast tapestry of the American food industry, regulatory authorities stand as the pillars of safety, quality, and compliance. Their influence extends from the farm to the dinner table, ensuring that the nation's food supply remains among the safest in the world. This section offers an in-depth exploration of these major regulatory bodies, their historical contexts, and the breadth of their oversight.

The U.S. Department of Agriculture (USDA)

Founded in 1862 by President Abraham Lincoln, the USDA is an expansive federal agency that oversees numerous aspects of American agriculture. However, when it comes to food safety, a specific branch of the USDA, the Food Safety and Inspection Service (FSIS), takes the lead. The FSIS is responsible for ensuring the safety and proper labeling of meat, poultry, and processed egg products.

The USDA also administers several other programs related to food, such as the National Organic Program, which sets and verifies standards for organic agricultural products, and the Supplemental Nutrition Assistance Program (SNAP), which provides nutritional assistance to eligible individuals and families.

The Food and Drug Administration (FDA)

Established in 1906 following the passage of the Pure Food and Drugs Act, the FDA is a part of the U.S. Department of Health and Human Services. This agency is tasked with the regulation of a wide variety of products, including foods (other than those under USDA's purview), drugs, medical devices, and cosmetics.

For the food industry, the FDA's jurisdiction is vast, covering dairy products, seafood, fruits, vegetables, and more. The FDA ensures these products are safe, wholesome, and correctly labeled. In recent years, the FDA has been instrumental in rolling out the Food Safety Modernization Act (FSMA), a transformative piece of legislation aimed at shifting the focus from reacting to foodborne illness outbreaks to preventing them.

The Environmental Protection Agency (EPA)

While not exclusively a food regulatory body, the EPA plays a crucial role in maintaining food safety. Founded in 1970, the agency's primary responsibility is the protection of human health and the environment. In the context of the food industry, the EPA regulates the use of pesticides and sets tolerance levels for pesticide residues on food, ensuring that they remain within limits that have been scientifically verified as safe. The EPA also oversees water quality standards, which directly impacts the safety of the water used in food production and processing.

The Centers for Disease Control and Prevention (CDC)

A division of the U.S. Department of Health and Human Services, the CDC, established in 1946, is primarily known for its work in disease monitoring and prevention. When it comes to food safety, the CDC plays a crucial surveillance role. It monitors and investigates outbreaks of foodborne illnesses, working closely with state and local health departments. While the CDC doesn't regulate food products, its work in identifying and controlling foodborne disease outbreaks is vital in shaping food safety policies and practices.

The Alcohol and Tobacco Tax and Trade Bureau (TTB)

Within the U.S. Department of the Treasury, the TTB holds the responsibility of regulating the production, distribution, labeling, and advertising of alcoholic beverages, ensuring they conform to U.S. laws and regulations.

While its scope might be more limited compared to other regulatory bodies, the TTB's role in overseeing one segment of consumable products makes it an essential player in the broader food regulatory landscape.

6.2 Key Regulations and Guidelines

The myriad of regulations and guidelines governing the food industry in the USA can be overwhelming, especially for newcomers or those branching into new areas of food production and sales. These rules serve as foundational pillars to ensure that food remains safe, of high quality, and free from fraudulent practices. Though it's impossible to cover every regulation in detail within this scope, we'll delve into some of the most influential and significant ones that industry stakeholders should be well-versed with.

The Pure Food and Drug Act of 1906

The genesis of food regulation in the United States can be traced back to the Pure Food and Drug Act. This landmark legislation prohibited the sale of misbranded or adulterated food and drugs. It set the stage for the establishment of the Food and Drug Administration (FDA) and provided the initial momentum for the federal government to take an active role in food safety and labeling.

The Federal Meat Inspection Act of 1906

Enacted concurrently with the Pure Food and Drug Act, this statute mandated the inspection of meat processing and slaughterhouses to ensure the meat and meat products' sanitary and safety conditions. Under the U.S. Department of Agriculture's purview, it primarily aimed to prevent adulterated or misbranded meat from reaching consumers.

The Food Safety Modernization Act (FSMA) of 2011

Arguably one of the most transformative pieces of food legislation in recent decades, FSMA shifted the focus of the U.S. food safety system from responding to contamination events to preventing them. The Act introduced several new regulations, including mandates for food facilities to implement preventive controls, importers to verify foreign suppliers' safety, and the establishment of safety standards for produce farms.

The Nutrition Labeling and Education Act of 1990

Before this act's enactment, nutrition labeling was voluntary and not standardized. This legislation mandated nutrition labeling on most food products and standardized the format, ensuring consumers received consistent and accurate nutritional information. It established what could be considered a "low fat" or "high fiber" product, for instance, and ensured claims were backed by evidence.

The Pesticide Residue Amendment of 1954

Linked to the Federal Food, Drug, and Cosmetic Act, this amendment set tolerances for pesticide residues on raw agricultural products. It recognized the reality that certain pesticide residues might remain on food, even after thorough washing or cooking. The amendment aimed to ensure that these residues, if present, were within scientifically determined safe levels.

The Egg Products Inspection Act of 1970

Eggs and egg products, while nutritious, are potential carriers of harmful pathogens. Recognizing this risk, this Act mandated the inspection of egg processing facilities, ensuring that eggs sold to consumers were fresh and free from discernible defects. It also led to the establishment of sanitary standards for these facilities.

Seafood HACCP Regulation of 1995

HACCP, or Hazard Analysis Critical Control Point, is a management system that addresses food safety through the analysis and control of potential hazards. The Seafood HACCP regulation was groundbreaking as it was the first time HACCP principles were applied to a specific food sector. It mandated seafood processors to identify hazards associated with their products and processes and implement controls at critical points to prevent, reduce, or eliminate those hazards.

Bioterrorism Act of 2002

In a post-9/11 world, ensuring the security of the nation's food supply became paramount. This Act introduced measures to protect the food supply from potential acts of bioterrorism. Key provisions included the requirement for food facilities to register with the FDA and establish records that allow for the tracking and tracing of food products.

6.3 Inspection Procedures

Inspections and audits are integral components of the U.S. food safety and regulatory framework. They serve as a tool for enforcing compliance with established regulations and provide a direct line of feedback to food business operators on their practices, operations, and standards. As such, it's imperative for those in the industry to be well-prepared and knowledgeable about what to expect during these reviews.

At their core, inspections are about ensuring public safety. The main objective is to verify that food is being produced, processed, and sold in a manner that meets the established safety standards. It's a proactive measure that helps to prevent outbreaks of foodborne illnesses, misbranding, and other violations that could pose a threat to consumers.

Types of Inspections

Inspections come in different forms, each tailored to specific sectors or purposes:

- **Routine Inspections:** These are scheduled checks that regulatory bodies carry out to ensure ongoing compliance with food safety standards. Depending on the nature of the business and its history of compliance, these can be annual, biannual, or even more frequent.

- **Complaint-driven Inspections:** If a consumer or another party lodges a complaint about a particular establishment, this can trigger an inspection. Such reviews are typically unscheduled and can occur at any time.

- **Follow-up Inspections:** If a business has been found non-compliant in a previous inspection, a follow-up visit is conducted to ensure that corrective actions have been taken.

- **Sampling Inspections:** Here, inspectors focus on taking samples of food products to be analyzed in a laboratory setting for contaminants, adulterants, or other potential hazards.

The Inspection Process

Though the exact procedure might vary slightly based on the inspecting authority and the nature of the business, the general process remains somewhat consistent:

1. **Notification:** Depending on the type of inspection, establishments might receive prior notice. However, unannounced inspections are also common, especially for complaint-driven or follow-up inspections.

2. **Opening Conference:** The inspector meets with the facility's manager or designated representative to explain the purpose, scope, and process of the inspection. This provides clarity and sets the stage for a smooth in-

spection.

3. **Physical Inspection:** The inspector conducts a walk-through of the facility, observing practices, conditions, and operations. They might review storage areas, processing lines, equipment, and even staff behavior.

4. **Document Review:** The inspector will review essential records, such as temperature logs, sanitation records, employee training logs, and other documents relevant to ensuring food safety compliance.

5. **Sampling:** If deemed necessary, the inspector might collect samples for further analysis.

6. **Closing Conference:** At the conclusion of the inspection, the inspector meets again with the facility's representative to discuss preliminary findings, observations, and potential violations. This is an opportunity for the establishment to seek clarification and understand any necessary corrective actions.

Preparing for an Inspection

A proactive approach is the best strategy:

Maintain Regular Internal Audits: Establish a schedule for internal audits to identify and rectify issues before an official inspection.

Train Staff: Employees should be adequately trained on food safety protocols, personal hygiene, and other relevant regulations.

Keep Records Up-to-date: Organized and current records can expedite the inspection process and demonstrate your commitment to compliance.

Facilitate the Inspector: Ensure that the inspector has access to all necessary areas and documents. Cooperation can help in building a positive rapport.

Potential Outcomes of an Inspection

After an inspection, the establishment might receive:

- **A Clean Bill of Health:** Indicating that no significant issues were identified.
- **Minor Violations:** These require corrective action but might not pose immediate threats.
- **Major Violations:** Indicating a significant breach of regulations, which might result in penalties, further inspections, or even temporary closure until issues are resolved.

6.4 Handling Non-compliances and Penalties

Non-compliance refers to the failure of an establishment or entity to adhere to the rules, regulations, and standards set by regulatory bodies. These can range from minor infractions, like paperwork omissions, to major ones, such as contamination that could pose significant health risks. The nature and gravity of the non-compliance will typically dictate the severity of penalties and the course of action required.

Immediate Steps After Non-compliance Detection

Acknowledgment and Rectification: The first step in handling non-compliances is acknowledgment. Denial or ignorance can exacerbate the situation. Once a non-compliance is identified, immediate steps should be taken to rectify it. For example, if a contaminant is detected in a food product, the immediate course of action would be to halt production and recall affected products.

Engage with Regulatory Authorities: Open channels of communication with the concerned regulatory body. This demonstrates a willingness to cooperate and rectify issues. Often, regulatory bodies will provide guidelines or support in addressing the non-compliance, ensuring it is handled adequately.

Document Everything: Whether it's the nature of the non-compliance, the steps taken to address it, or communications with regulatory bodies—documentation is paramount. This not only provides a record of actions but can also be crucial if legal actions arise.

Penalties and Their Implications

The penalties for non-compliances vary, predicated on the severity of the infraction and the risk posed to the public. Some potential penalties include:

1. **Fines:** Monetary penalties are common, especially for minor infractions. The amount can vary, often determined by the nature of the non-compliance and its potential impact.
2. **Suspensions:** For more severe infractions, an establishment's license or permit might be temporarily suspended. This could mean a halt in operations until the non-compliance is addressed.
3. **Revocations:** In extreme cases, where there's a consistent history of non-compliance or a severe risk to public safety, licenses or permits might be permanently revoked.
4. **Legal Proceedings:** Non-compliances posing significant risks or resulting in harm can lead to legal proceedings, where the establishment may face lawsuits or criminal charges.

Navigating Penalties and Building a Way Forward

- Legal Counsel: If faced with penalties, especially severe ones, it's advisable to engage with legal counsel familiar with food industry regulations. They can provide guidance on rights, potential defenses, and negotiation pathways.

- Review and Strengthen Internal Processes: Use the incident as an opportunity to review internal processes, training protocols, and checks. This not only prevents future non-compliances but also demonstrates a commitment to upholding standards.

- Transparency with Stakeholders: Be transparent with stakeholders, including customers, suppliers, and partners. This helps in retaining trust and also underscores the commitment to rectifying mistakes.

- Regular Compliance Checks: Implement regular internal audits and compliance checks. Being proactive can prevent many non-compliances from occurring in the first place.

6.5 Useful Resources

Navigating the intricate maze of regulatory standards and requirements in the food service industry necessitates not only a deep understanding of the rules but also access to timely updates and additional resources. While this manual aims to provide a comprehensive overview, it's also crucial for industry professionals to be proactive in seeking out current, reliable, and pertinent information from trusted sources. In this section, we delve into an array of resources that serve as reservoirs of knowledge and guidance for those in the U.S. food service sector.

Government Websites and Databases

The U.S. Food and Drug Administration (FDA): The FDA's website is a treasure trove of information. From detailed regulations to recent updates, recalls, and safety alerts, the FDA offers a wide range of resources.

Additionally, they have a dedicated section for the food industry that includes guidelines, compliance, and regulatory information. Subscribing to the FDA's news releases or following their official social media channels can also keep professionals abreast of the latest developments.

The U.S. Department of Agriculture (USDA): The USDA oversees many aspects of food safety, especially concerning meat, poultry, and processed egg products. Their website offers resources ranging from inspection services to recent research and data. The USDA's Food Safety and Inspection Service (FSIS) also provides publications, industry guidelines, and relevant news.

Centers for Disease Control and Prevention (CDC): While the CDC's primary focus is on public health, they offer vital information on foodborne illnesses, outbreaks, and preventive measures. Their research and reports can provide valuable insights into food safety trends and challenges.

Trade Associations and Organizations

Several trade associations and organizations cater to the food service industry, providing resources, training, updates, and networking opportunities.

The National Restaurant Association: As one of the largest food service trade organizations in the U.S., the National Restaurant Association provides a plethora of resources for its members, including research, training tools, and regulatory updates.

The Food Marketing Institute (FMI): Catering primarily to the supermarket and grocery sectors, FMI provides research, publications, and policy position updates relevant to food retailers and wholesalers.

The Institute of Food Technologists (IFT): For those more inclined towards the scientific and technological aspects of food, IFT provides resources on research, innovation, and industry trends.

Publications and Industry Journals

Several reputable publications and journals focus on the food industry, offering in-depth articles, research, and insights.

Food Safety Magazine: This bimonthly publication delves deep into food safety challenges, strategies, and solutions. It offers both practical insights and academic research.

The Journal of Food Protection: A peer-reviewed monthly publication, this journal covers the gamut of food safety and protection topics, from microbial hazards to chemical contaminants.

Food Quality & Safety Magazine: Beyond just safety, this magazine addresses broader quality concerns in the food industry, offering insights into best practices, trends, and solutions.

6.6 Continuing Education

In the dynamic realm of the food service industry, change is the only constant. From emerging foodborne pathogens and changing consumer preferences to novel technologies and updated regulations, the industry is perpetually in flux. Against this backdrop, the role of continuing education takes on heightened significance. For industry professionals, be they chefs, restaurant managers, food suppliers, or quality assurance personnel, the commitment to lifelong learning is not merely a means to remain relevant but is a professional obligation, ensuring the safety, quality, and sustainability of the food products they provide to the public.

The Impetus for Continuing Education

Evolving Regulatory Landscape: As discussed in previous sections, the food service industry in the USA is governed by a variety of regulatory bodies, each with its own set of rules, standards, and guidelines. These regulations are not static. They evolve, reflecting new scientific knowledge, public health data, technological advancements, and societal demands. Staying abreast of these changes is essential for compliance, which in turn prevents costly penalties, ensures customer trust, and safeguards public health.

Technological Advancements: The last few decades have witnessed revolutionary changes in how food is produced, processed, distributed, and consumed. From precision agriculture and genetic modifications to smart kitchen appliances and food delivery apps, technology has reshaped the industry. These innovations bring about new opportunities, challenges, and risks. Only through continuous learning can professionals harness these technologies' potential while mitigating their drawbacks.

Consumer Dynamics: Today's consumers are more informed, discerning, and demanding than ever before. Concerns about health and wellness, sustainability, ethics, and authenticity drive purchasing decisions. By dedicating themselves to ongoing education, food service professionals can anticipate, understand, and meet these ever-shifting consumer expectations, thereby ensuring customer loyalty and business success.

Emerging Food Safety Challenges: New foodborne diseases, evolving pathogens, globalized supply chains, and changing climatic conditions pose fresh challenges to food safety. Being proactive in updating one's knowledge and skills is paramount in preemptively addressing these issues, thereby upholding the industry's primary commitment to safety.

Frameworks for Continuing Education

Continuing education in the food service industry is facilitated by a host of structured and unstructured avenues:

Certification Programs: Many institutions and industry bodies offer certification programs tailored for various specializations within the food service sector. These programs, often culminating in an examination, ensure that professionals are conversant with the latest standards and practices.

Workshops and Seminars: Regularly organized by trade associations, regulatory bodies, and academic institutions, these events provide focused learning on specific topics, ranging from novel cooking techniques to the intricacies of a new regulation.

Academic Courses: For those looking to delve deeper, many universities and colleges offer undergraduate, postgraduate, and doctoral programs in food science, culinary arts, food business, and related fields. These formal education pathways provide both foundational knowledge and specialized expertise.

Online Platforms: Platforms like Coursera, Udemy, and edX offer courses on a plethora of food-related topics. Webinars, podcasts, and online workshops further supplement this virtual learning ecosystem.

Industry Publications: Subscribing to journals, magazines, and newsletters specific to the food industry ensures a steady stream of updated knowledge. Not only do these publications provide insights into recent developments, but they also stimulate thought by presenting different perspectives on contentious issues.

Chapter 7: Advanced Cooking Techniques and Food Technologies

7.1 Sous-vide Cooking

Sous-vide, a French term translating to "under vacuum," is a unique and advanced culinary method that has gained notable attention in the past few decades. Rooted in the principles of precision and consistency, sous-vide cooking involves sealing food in an airtight bag and submerging it in a water bath at a specific, controlled temperature. This ensures that the food cooks uniformly without any part being over or undercooked. For those seeking Food Manager Certification, understanding the intricacies and safety protocols of this method is vital.

The appeal of sous-vide lies in its ability to consistently produce results that are often difficult to achieve through traditional cooking methods. For instance, a steak can be cooked to a perfect medium-rare throughout its thickness, without the risk of overcooking the outer layers. Similarly, delicate foods like fish or vegetables retain their texture and nutrients without being subjected to high, direct heat.

However, the advantages of sous-vide also come with certain responsibilities, especially in a professional setting where food safety is paramount.

Temperature Control: One of the fundamental principles of sous-vide cooking is precise temperature control. Traditional cooking methods often involve higher temperatures, which kill harmful bacteria relatively quickly. With sous-vide, the cooking temperatures are typically lower, often hovering around the desired final internal temperature of the food. As such, understanding the time-temperature relationship is crucial. Extended periods at controlled temperatures ensure the reduction of bacteria to safe levels. For instance, while salmonella can be killed at 165°F in seconds, at 136°F, it might require a longer time, like 68.4 minutes.

Packaging and Oxygen: Food, when vacuum-sealed, has the oxygen removed from its environment. This anaerobic environment can be conducive to the growth of certain pathogens, such as Clostridium botulinum, which produces the botulin toxin. While this bacterium is killed at high temperatures, its spores can survive and may germinate in oxygen-free environments that are between 38°F and 126°F. As a preventive measure, foods cooked sous-vide should either be served immediately, rapidly cooled and refrigerated, or held at temperatures above 130°F to prevent spore germination.

Rapid Cooling and Storage: Post sous-vide cooking, if the food isn't served immediately, it's crucial to cool it rapidly to prevent bacterial growth. This is typically done by plunging the vacuum-sealed bag into an ice bath. Once cooled, the food can be refrigerated and later reheated safely. Always remember the golden rule: the time food spends in the temperature "danger zone" (between 41°F and 135°F) should be minimized.

Equipment Maintenance: Maintaining the equipment used in sous-vide cooking is paramount. Water bath circulators should be regularly checked for accuracy using a calibrated thermometer. Vacuum sealers should be inspected to ensure they are sealing bags correctly, and the integrity of the seals should always be confirmed before cooking. An improper seal can introduce air into the bag, disrupting the cooking process and posing potential safety risks.

Reheating: When reheating sous-vide-cooked foods, it's important to bring them back to their initial cooking temperature or higher to ensure safety. Rapid reheating methods are preferred to minimize the time food spends in the "danger zone."

7.2 Fermentation and Preservation

Fermentation and preservation represent two time-honored techniques in the culinary and food management worlds. They not only contribute unique flavors, textures, and aromas to foods but also play a pivotal role in extending shelf life and enhancing the nutritional profile of many products. As individuals aspire to achieve their Food Manager Certification, gaining a nuanced understanding of these methods, especially in the context of safety and regulatory requirements, becomes paramount.

At its core, fermentation is a metabolic process where microorganisms such as bacteria, yeast, and molds break down food components (like sugars and starches) into other products. Depending on the microorganism and conditions, this can result in alcohol, lactic acid, or other compounds.

Benefits of Fermentation:

1. **Flavor Development:** Fermentation imparts unique flavors to foods. The tang of sauerkraut, the sourness of yogurt, and the complex profiles of fermented beverages like wine or beer are all results of fermentation.

2. **Nutritional Enhancement:** Fermented foods can have enhanced nutritional profiles. The process can increase the availability of vitamins and minerals, produce beneficial enzymes, and even create health-promoting probiotic bacteria.

3. **Natural Preservation:** The acidic environment created during fermentation can act as a natural preservative, deterring the growth of harmful bacteria.

Safety Considerations

Correct Microorganisms: Utilizing the right starter cultures or ensuring the right environment for beneficial wild microorganisms is crucial. Undesirable or harmful microbes can compromise both the product's safety and quality.

Appropriate Salt and Acid Levels: Many fermentations, especially vegetable ones like pickles or kimchi, rely on salt. Salt not only flavors the food but also selects for lactic acid bacteria over potential pathogens. Monitoring acidity ensures that the environment remains inhospitable to harmful microbes.

Preservation: Preservation methods aim to extend the shelf life of foods by halting the growth of microorganisms or by killing them outright. Some methods also inhibit enzymatic reactions that can degrade food quality.

Common Preservation Techniques

Canning: This involves placing foods in jars or cans and heating them to destroy microorganisms. Once sealed, the absence of oxygen and the acidic or sugar-rich environment inside the can or jar prevent the growth of spoilage organisms and pathogens.

Drying: Removing moisture from food inhibits the growth of microorganisms. Dried foods, such as jerky or dried fruits, have been staples for millennia.

Cold Storage: Refrigeration and freezing slow down microbial growth and enzymatic reactions. While freezing can halt most microbial activity, refrigeration merely reduces it.

Safety Considerations:

Botulism Concerns: In canning, especially low-acid foods, there's a risk of Clostridium botulinum spores surviving and producing botulin toxin in the anaerobic environment of the can or jar. It's essential to follow tested canning procedures and, for many low-acid foods, to use pressure canning.

Rehydration Caution: When rehydrating dried foods, it's vital to handle them as perishables and to refrigerate any leftovers immediately.

Freezer Burn: While not a safety concern, freezer burn can degrade the quality of frozen foods. Proper packaging can prevent this.

7.3 Modernist Cuisine and Molecular Gastronomy

Originating in the late 20th century, modernist cuisine represents an approach to cooking that utilizes innovative tools, ingredients, and methods, many borrowed or adapted from industrial food processing or research labs. Techniques like sous-vide cooking, which we previously discussed, fall under this category. The term itself gained significant attention from the monumental work "Modernist Cuisine: The Art and Science of Cooking" by Nathan Myhrvold.

Key Features of modern cuisine are:

Equipment Innovation: Modernist cuisine often employs cutting-edge kitchen gadgets such as immersion circulators, centrifuges, and rotary evaporators.

Ingredient Exploration: Ingredients unfamiliar to the traditional kitchen, like hydrocolloids, emulsifying agents, and specialized proteins, are common in modernist cuisine.

The term **"molecular gastronomy"** denotes the scientific study of culinary phenomena, essentially focusing on the 'why' of cooking. Pioneered by figures like Hervé This and Nicholas Kurti, molecular gastronomy seeks to understand the changes that ingredients undergo during cooking at a molecular level.

Key Features of molecular gastronomy are:

Texture Transformation: Techniques like spherification, which encapsulates a liquid within a gel-like membrane, or the use of foaming agents to create culinary foams, showcase the transformative power of molecular gastronomy.

Flavor Pairing: Using scientific data, chefs can pair ingredients with complementary flavor compounds, leading to unexpected yet delightful combinations.

Safety Considerations for Modernist Cuisine and Molecular Gastronomy

1. Ingredient Sourcing: Given the specialized nature of many ingredients used, it's crucial to source high-quality, food-grade substances. Some chemicals, while having a culinary application, can be hazardous in larger quantities or if sourced from non-food-grade suppliers.

2. Equipment Handling: The equipment used can often be more intricate and potentially hazardous than traditional kitchen tools. Proper training and handling are imperative to avoid injuries.

3. Temperature Monitoring: As with sous-vide cooking, precise temperature control is essential for both safety and achieving desired culinary outcomes. Ensuring equipment is calibrated and functioning correctly is a must.

4. Relevance to Food Manager Certification: With an increasing number of establishments exploring the boundaries of culinary art through modernist cuisine and molecular gastronomy, food managers need to be adept at understanding the nuances these methods bring. This includes:

- Ensuring staff training for specialized equipment and techniques.
- Rigorous monitoring of ingredient storage and sourcing to maintain safety standards.
- Keeping updated with regulatory standards pertaining to novel in-

gredients and methods.

7.4 Food Pairing Based on Science

In the vast panorama of culinary arts, the pairing of foods has always been integral to creating harmonious and delicious dishes. Traditionally, such combinations were born out of cultural preferences, regional ingredients, and centuries of culinary evolution. However, as the barriers between science and cooking become more porous, we are witnessing the rise of food pairings based on scientific principles. Understanding the underpinnings of this approach can prove invaluable for those seeking a Food Manager Certification, especially when considering the safety, efficiency, and innovation aspects of food management.

At the heart of scientific food pairing lies the study of aroma compounds. Every food item contains volatile and non-volatile molecules that contribute to its unique flavor profile. By analyzing these compounds and comparing them between different foods, scientists can predict which ingredients might pair well together based on shared or complementary molecular profiles.

Key Components of Scientific Food Pairing

1. **Flavor Compound Analysis**: Advanced techniques such as gas chromatography and mass spectrometry are employed to identify and quantify the volatile compounds present in foods. This data becomes the foundation for scientifically-informed pairing decisions.
2. **Database Compilation:** As researchers amass information on the flavor compounds of various foods, extensive databases are being built. These resources, some of which are accessible online, can guide chefs and food professionals in creating innovative pairings.
3. **Sensory Perception:** Beyond just molecular compatibility, the human perception of flavors plays a vital role. Factors like taste receptors, olfactory response, and even psychological influences impact how paired foods are experienced by diners.

Safety and Efficiency Considerations

Novel Ingredients: Scientific food pairing may lead to the use of uncommon or novel ingredients. As a food manager, one must ensure that these ingredients meet all safety standards and are stored and handled correctly.

Consistency: With scientific food pairing, dishes can achieve a level of consistency in flavor, given that they are based on quantifiable data. This can enhance the efficiency of food preparation and reduce waste.

Allergens and Dietary Restrictions: As new and unexpected ingredients find their way onto plates, food managers need to be acutely aware of potential allergens or dietary incompatibilities.

Relevance to Food Manager Certification

1. Menu Development: Scientific food pairing can be an asset for food establishments looking to stand out and offer unique dishes. Managers can collaborate with chefs to incorporate these principles into menu development.

2. Customer Experience: Offering scientifically-paired dishes can elevate the dining experience, leading to greater customer satisfaction and repeat business.

3. Ongoing Education: As the field is continually evolving, staying updated with the latest research and findings in scientific food pairing can give an edge to food managers and their establishments.

7.5 Technology in the Kitchen: Smart Appliances

The modern kitchen is undergoing a rapid transformation, with technology playing a pivotal role in redefining how we approach food preparation and management. As food service professionals strive for efficiency, consistency, and safety, integrating smart appliances into the kitchen can be a game-changer. For those pursuing a Food Manager Certification, an understanding of these technological innovations is crucial, especially in the context of ensuring optimal operational efficiency and maintaining the highest standards of food safety.

Smart appliances are devices integrated with advanced electronics and, often, internet connectivity. This allows them to perform their primary functions with enhanced precision, automation, and user-friendly interfaces. Furthermore, their "smart" designation often implies a degree of interactivity with other devices or centralized management systems.

Key Smart Appliances Revolutionizing Kitchens

1. **Smart Ovens and Stovetops:** Modern ovens and stovetops come with features like precise temperature control, pre-programmed cooking modes for specific dishes, and remote monitoring via smartphone applications. Some even have internal cameras, allowing chefs to monitor cooking progress without opening the oven door.

2. **Smart Refrigerators**: These refrigerators can track inventory, monitor expiration dates, adjust cooling zones based on content, and even offer touch-screen interfaces for recipe suggestions or order grocery items.

3. **Precision Cookers:** Devices designed for methods like sous-vide, these cookers allow for exact temperature settings, ensuring consistent results every time.

4. **Smart Dishwashers:** With sensors to detect the level of grime and adjust the wash cycle accordingly, these dishwashers optimize water usage and ensure thorough cleaning.

Implications for Food Management

Safety Enhancements: Smart appliances often come with built-in safety features. For instance, a smart stovetop might turn off automatically if no cookware is detected for a set period, preventing potential fires. Similarly, smart refrigerators monitoring temperature fluctuations can alert managers to potential malfunctions, safeguarding against food spoilage.

Efficiency and Consistency: Automated and precision-focused features of these appliances ensure that dishes are prepared consistently, reducing the margin of error. This not only leads to a better dining experience for patrons but also optimizes resource usage.

Data Collection and Analytics: Many smart appliances can collect data on usage patterns, energy consumption, and more. This data can be invaluable for food managers in making informed decisions about menu adjustments, energy-saving measures, and equipment maintenance.

Staff Training: With the introduction of technology in the kitchen, there's a need for staff to be adequately trained. Food managers should ensure that their team is comfortable with these devices, understands their functionalities, and can troubleshoot basic issues.

Relevance to Food Manager Certification

Operational Oversight: As kitchens become more tech-centric, managers need to be adept at overseeing a blend of traditional culinary skills and modern technological operations. This requires a nuanced understanding of both realms.

Maintenance and Upgrades: Smart appliances, being technology products, will require periodic software updates, maintenance, and sometimes hardware repairs. Managers should be proactive in ensuring that these devices are always in optimal working condition.

Budgeting and Investment: High-tech appliances can be a significant investment. Food managers should be able to assess the long-term benefits, ROI, and potential savings of integrating such devices into the kitchen.

Chapter 8: Dietary Restrictions and Food Ethics

8.1 Vegetarian and Vegan Diets

The world of gastronomy is as diverse as the cultures it stems from, continuously evolving to cater to the broad spectrum of human preferences and ethical considerations. Among these multifaceted inclinations, vegetarianism and veganism have emerged not just as dietary choices, but as profound statements on health, environment, and animal rights. As the culinary world acknowledges these choices, the importance of understanding them becomes paramount.

Vegetarianism and veganism are often used interchangeably, but they represent distinct dietary practices:

Vegetarian Diet: A diet that excludes meat, poultry, and seafood. However, it may include dairy products and eggs. There are further subdivisions like lacto-vegetarians (consume dairy but not eggs), ovo-vegetarians (consume eggs but not dairy), and lacto-ovo vegetarians (consume both dairy and eggs).

Vegan Diet: A stricter form of vegetarianism, it excludes all animal products, including dairy, eggs, and even honey. It often extends beyond diet to exclude any products derived from animals, such as leather or wool.

Relevance to Food Management

1. Menu Planning: Recognizing the growth of vegetarian and vegan patrons, it becomes essential for restaurants to provide a diverse range of options. This not only caters to the dietary restrictions but also ensures that the offerings are nutritious, fulfilling, and in line with the ethical considerations of the diners.

2. Cross-contamination Concerns: Just as allergens require careful handling, so too do vegetarian and vegan dishes. Utensils, surfaces, and even frying oils must be separate to ensure that there's no contact with meat or other non-vegetarian items. For vegans, even dairy and eggs are potential contaminants.

3. Ingredient Sourcing: A significant part of managing a food establishment is sourcing ingredients. For vegetarian and vegan dishes, this goes beyond ensuring the absence of meat. Managers must ensure that items like rennet (often used in cheese production and derived from animal stomachs) or gelatin (derived from animal bones and used in many desserts) are replaced with vegetarian or vegan alternatives.

4. Nutritional Balance: Vegetarian and vegan diets, while healthy, require careful planning to ensure all necessary nutrients are provided. For example, certain nutrients predominantly found in meats, such as Vitamin B12 or iron, need to be sourced from alternative ingredients or supplemented.

5. Training and Awareness: Staff, especially those interacting with patrons, should be knowledgeable about what constitutes a vegetarian or vegan dish. They should be prepared to answer queries and accommodate special requests.

Implications for Food Manager Certification

For those pursuing a Food Manager Certification, understanding the intricacies of vegetarian and vegan diets is not just about respecting personal choices. It has deeper implications:

- Regulatory Compliance: Some states have regulations and guidelines concerning the clear labeling of vegetarian and vegan options and ensuring that they are genuinely free of animal-derived ingredients.

- Safety Protocols: Just as cross-contamination can be a concern for allergens, similar care must be taken for vegetarian and vegan dishes. This is especially true in buffets or shared kitchen spaces.

- Ethical Considerations: As with sourcing sustainably caught fish or ethically raised meats, ensuring the authenticity of vegetarian and vegan dishes speaks to the integrity of a food establishment.

- Economic Impact: With a growing segment of the population choosing vegetarian or vegan diets, accommodating these diets is not just ethically right but also economically sound. Such inclusion can expand the customer base and ensure repeat business.

8.2 Religious Dietary Laws: Halal, Kosher, etc.

8.2 Religious Dietary Laws: Halal, Kosher, etc.

Religious dietary laws are a testament to the deep connection between food and spiritual beliefs. Adherence to these laws is not merely about following a set of rules, but it reflects a broader sense of devotion, discipline, and cultural identity. For those in the food industry, particularly those aiming for the Food Manager Certification, a comprehension of these dietary requirements is indispensable. Such knowledge ensures respect for diverse clientele, compliance with regulatory standards, and the establishment of trust among consumers.

Key Religious Dietary Laws

1. Halal:

Derived from the Arabic word meaning “permissible,” Halal refers to what is allowable under Islamic law. Central to Halal dietary practices are:

- Prohibition of pork and its by-products.
- Only specific methods of animal slaughter, deemed 'Zabiha', are permissible. The name of God must be invoked at the time of slaughtering.
- Alcohol and intoxicants are forbidden.
- Processing, preparation, and storage equipment should be free from any haram (prohibited) elements.

2. Kosher:

Kosher is a term used to describe food that complies with traditional Jewish dietary law - kashrut.

- Meat and dairy cannot be mixed or consumed together.
- Only certain animals, those that chew cud and have split hooves, like cows and sheep, are permissible.
- Animals must be slaughtered in a precise manner under rabbinical supervision.
- Shellfish and certain seafood are prohibited.
- Utensils and kitchen appliances used for meat cannot be used for dairy and vice versa.

3. Hindu Dietary Practices:

While Hinduism encompasses a wide range of practices, some key dietary principles are:

- Many Hindus abstain from eating beef since the cow is considered sacred.
- Some Hindus are vegetarian, excluding all meat and fish.
- Consumption of alcohol might be restricted or prohibited among some sects.

4. Buddhist Dietary Laws:

Many Buddhists follow a vegetarian or vegan diet, refraining from consuming any animals.

Specific sects might avoid certain pungent vegetables like garlic and onions, believing they increase passion.

Implications for Food Managers

1. Menu Diversity: To cater to a diverse clientele, restaurants and food service establishments can offer a selection of dishes that comply with various religious dietary laws. Having certified Halal or Kosher dishes can attract and satisfy a wider audience.

2. Certification and Labeling: Various organizations provide Halal and Kosher certifications, ensuring that the products or dishes adhere to the respective religious laws. Having these certifications and displaying them prominently can instill confidence in consumers.

3. Training and Awareness: Ensuring staff, especially those in direct contact with patrons, are knowledgeable about these dietary requirements can enhance the dining experience for many. It's not just about serving the right food but also about answering questions and making suitable recommendations.

4. Avoid Cross-Contamination: Just as with vegetarian or vegan preparations, care must be taken to ensure that foods adhering to religious dietary laws are not contaminated. This might mean separate storage, distinct utensils, or even dedicated preparation areas.

5. Economic Implications: There's a growing demand for Halal and Kosher products globally. Tapping into this market can mean increased revenue. Moreover, patrons often show loyalty to establishments that cater to

their dietary requirements with authenticity and respect.

6. Regulatory Standards: In certain areas, there might be regulations regarding the labeling and authenticity of Halal or Kosher foods. Adherence to these standards is not just about legal compliance but also about establishing trust.

8.3 Ethical Sourcing: Fair Trade and Beyond

In today's globalized food market, where ingredients can be sourced from across the world, the journey of every food item from farm to fork has become more intricate than ever. As consumers become more conscious of their choices and their implications, the need for ethically sourced products has skyrocketed. But what does it mean to source ethically, and why is it crucial for food managers to incorporate this into their management approach?

At its core, ethical sourcing involves obtaining products in a responsible and sustainable way, ensuring that the workers involved in its production are treated with fairness, respect, and dignity. This means providing adequate wages, ensuring safe working conditions, prohibiting child labor, and adopting sustainable practices that are environmentally friendly.

Fair Trade: The Gold Standard

The Fair Trade movement has been at the forefront of advocating for ethically produced goods, especially in the domains of coffee, tea, cocoa, and sugar. By purchasing Fair Trade products, businesses ensure:

- Fair wages to the producers.
- Investment in local community projects.
- Environmentally sustainable farming practices.

However, Fair Trade is only a fraction of the broader ethical sourcing spectrum.

Beyond Fair Trade: Other Ethical Sourcing Considerations

1. Local and Organic Sourcing: Many establishments prioritize sourcing locally grown produce and ingredients, supporting local farmers and reducing carbon footprints associated with long-distance transportation. Organic sourcing also ensures that products are grown without harmful pesticides or genetically modified organisms.

2. Animal Welfare: Ethically sourced meat, poultry, and seafood mean that animals were treated humanely. Cage-free eggs, grass-fed beef, and sustainably caught fish are examples.

3. Reducing Food Waste: Adopting practices that minimize food wastage, whether by repurposing ingredients, donating excess food, or using composting methods, contributes to ethical food management.

4. Supporting Indigenous Communities: Sourcing products like quinoa, acai, or certain spices might involve engaging with indigenous communities. Ethical sourcing ensures they receive fair compensation and their traditions and lands are respected.

Implications for Food Managers

1. Building Trust with Consumers: Ethical sourcing resonates with many consumers who are keen on making socially responsible choices. By adopting such practices, establishments can foster trust and loyalty among patrons.

2. Regulatory Compliance: As concerns about unethical labor practices and environmental degradation intensify, regulations around transparent

and ethical sourcing may become stringent. Being proactive can help businesses stay ahead of the curve.

3. Economic Viability: While ethically sourced products might sometimes be pricier, they can command higher prices, particularly in markets where consumers value ethical considerations. Moreover, the long-term benefits of sustainable practices can offset initial costs.

4. Positive Brand Image: In the age of social media, a business's reputation is paramount. Ethical sourcing practices can enhance brand image and can be an essential part of marketing and promotional strategies.

8.4 Genetically Modified Foods: Pros and Cons

The debate over genetically modified (GM) foods has become one of the most polarizing issues in the world of food and agriculture. Genetically Modified Organisms (GMOs) refer to organisms whose genetic material has been altered in a way that does not occur naturally through mating or natural recombination. These modifications are designed to introduce a new trait to the organism which does not occur naturally in the species. Here, we delve into the pros and cons of GM foods to provide a holistic view on this controversial topic.

Pros of Genetically Modified Foods

- Enhanced Nutritional Content: Genetic modification can enhance the nutrient profile of foods. For example, Golden Rice is engineered to be rich in beta-carotene, a precursor to Vitamin A, potentially alleviating vitamin A deficiency in many populations.

- Higher Crop Yields: GMOs can be engineered to resist pests, tolerate harsh conditions, or grow faster. Such traits can lead to increased agricultural productivity.

- Reduced Dependency on Pesticides: Crops that are genetically modified to be pest-resistant can decrease the need for chemical pesticides, reducing environmental pollution.

- Extended Shelf Life: Genetic modifications can make fruits and vegetables more resistant to rotting or mechanical damage, leading to reduced food waste.

- Economic Benefits: Enhanced productivity and reduced dependency on pesticides can lead to increased profits for farmers.

- Potential for Biofortification: This involves enriching staple foods with essential nutrients, making them more nutritious. Such a technique could be revolutionary in addressing malnutrition.

Cons of Genetically Modified Foods

- Environmental Concerns: There are concerns about GMO crops crossbreeding with wild varieties, which can have unknown ecological consequences. The extensive planting of single crop varieties can also reduce biodiversity.

- Health Concerns: While numerous scientific studies have found that GM foods are safe for consumption, some worry about potential long-term health effects, allergies, and antibiotic resistance.

- Economic Implications: Patents on GM seeds can give biotech companies significant control over the food supply chain. This may result in increased seed prices and reduced autonomy for farmers.

- Ethical and Cultural Concerns: Some argue that manipulating the genetic code of organisms is "playing God" and raises moral questions. Additionally, certain communities and religions might have reservations about consuming GMOs based on their beliefs.

- Superweeds and Superbugs: Over-reliance on GMOs designed to resist pests or herbicides can lead to the evolution of superweeds and superbugs, which are harder to control.

- Labeling and Transparency Issues: Many consumers advocate for clear labeling of GM foods, allowing them to make informed choices. The debate around this topic continues, with industry players raising concerns about stigmatization.

For Food Managers: Implications and Responsibilities

Food managers need to be aware of the debates surrounding GMOs, not just from a production or sourcing standpoint but also considering consumer perception and demand. Here are some implications and responsibilities for food managers:

Sourcing Decisions: Deciding whether to source GM ingredients is a significant choice. This decision should factor in cost, consumer demand, regulatory compliance, and potential health and environmental implications.

Transparency: If an establishment decides to use GM ingredients, it is crucial to be transparent. This could involve clear labeling or even educating customers about the pros and cons of GMOs.

Continuous Education: The field of genetic modification is continually evolving. Food managers should stay updated on the latest research and regulatory changes related to GMOs.

Ethical Considerations: Managers should be sensitive to the cultural and ethical implications of serving GM foods and respect the dietary choices and concerns of their patrons.

8.5 Food Wastage and Ethical Disposal

Food waste is a pressing global concern with far-reaching environmental, economic, and ethical implications. The Food and Agriculture Organization (FAO) estimates that roughly one-third of the food produced globally goes to waste. In the context of the United States, this translates to approximately 133 billion pounds of food discarded annually.

Food waste can happen at various stages of the food supply chain and can involve production, processing or in some cases also distribution. The causes of food waste are multifaceted and can include:

- Aesthetic Standards: Supermarkets and consumers often reject perfectly edible food based on appearance alone.
- Inefficient Supply Chains: Breakdowns or inefficiencies can result in food spoiling before reaching consumers.
- Consumer Behavior: Over-purchasing, misunderstanding of expiration dates, and the undervaluing of food can lead to unnecessary waste.

The repercussions of food wastage are not just economic. When organic matter decomposes in landfills, it releases methane, a potent greenhouse gas that exacerbates climate change. Additionally, the water, energy, and resources invested in producing the wasted food are also squandered.

Ethical Disposal and Waste Reduction Strategies

1. For food managers, it is essential to recognize the role they play in curtailing this issue and implementing ethical disposal practices. Here are some strategies and practices they can employ:

2. Donations: One person's excess is another's essential. Collaborating with local food banks, shelters, and community organizations can help redirect excess food to those in need. Such practices not only reduce waste but also play a role in addressing food insecurity in communities.

3. Composting: Organic waste, when composted, can be transformed into nutrient-rich soil. Many establishments are now setting up on-site composting systems or partnering with local composting facilities. This reduces the load on landfills and recycles the waste into beneficial soil amendments.

4. Inventory Management: Smart inventory practices, like the FIFO (First In, First Out) system, can minimize spoilage. Advanced inventory software can also forecast demand, helping managers order optimally.

5. Educate Staff: Employees play a crucial role in reducing waste. Regular training sessions highlighting the importance of waste reduction, proper food storage, and efficient portioning can make a significant difference.

6. Consumer Awareness: Some food establishments have taken the initiative to educate consumers about food waste. This can be in the form of table-toppers highlighting waste statistics, suggesting taking leftovers home, or even offering portion size options.

7. Ethical Animal Byproduct Disposal: For establishments that handle meat, it's essential to ensure that animal byproducts are disposed of respecting local regulations and in a manner that minimizes environmental harm.

8. Collaboration with Suppliers: Building relationships with suppliers can pave the way for more flexible procurement practices. For instance, purchasing "ugly" fruits and vegetables at discounted rates not only reduces waste at the production level but can also lower costs for the establishment.

Chapter 9: Alcohol Management

9.1 Licensing and Regulations Related to Alcohol

The ability to serve and sell alcohol can greatly enhance the profitability of a food establishment, making it an essential facet for many managers to understand and navigate. However, the world of alcohol licensing and regulations is vast, complex, and varies not only from one country to another but often from one state or even city to the next. In the USA, the oversight and regulation of alcoholic beverages are primarily at the state level, and this means that food managers should have a comprehensive understanding of their particular state's laws and requirements.

Alcohol regulations in the United States have their roots in the 18th Amendment, which ushered in the Prohibition era (1920-1933). This amendment prohibited the manufacture, sale, and transportation of alcoholic beverages. However, with the 21st Amendment's ratification in 1933, Prohibition ended, and the power to regulate alcohol was handed back to the states. Each state was given the freedom to develop its system and regulations.

Today, each state has its own alcohol beverage control (ABC) board or commission responsible for granting licenses and permits, setting the terms for sales, and overseeing the enforcement of state liquor laws. While the details may vary, the underlying themes of these regulations are similar across states, focused on controlling distribution, preventing underage sales, and ensuring public safety.

Types of Licenses: Broadly, alcohol licenses can be categorized into on-premises and off-premises licenses. On-premises licenses are for establishments that want to sell alcohol for consumption at their location, such as restaurants, bars, or clubs. Off-premises licenses are for places selling alcohol to be consumed elsewhere, like liquor stores or grocery stores.

Licensing Considerations: The process to obtain an alcohol license generally involves several steps. An establishment must first ensure it meets zoning laws for their particular locale. There might be restrictions based on the establishment's proximity to schools, churches, or other public facilities. Once zoning is cleared, an establishment typically submits an application to the state's ABC board or commission. This application can be extensive, requiring details about the business, its owners, and its operation plans. A public notice period often follows, allowing community members to raise concerns or objections. Background checks, inspections, and fees are also common parts of the process.

Training Requirements: Given the potential legal and health risks associated with the sale of alcohol, many states mandate training programs for employees of licensed establishments. These programs, often referred to as responsible beverage service training, cover topics like checking identification, understanding alcohol's effects, and handling difficult situations, such as a patron who has had too much to drink.

Compliance and Penalties: After obtaining a license, the real work begins in terms of maintaining compliance with state and local laws. Regular checks and audits can be conducted by the regulatory authority. Non-compliance with regulations, such as serving minors or over-serving patrons, can result in severe penalties, including fines, license suspensions, or even revocations.

While the task of understanding and adhering to alcohol regulations might seem daunting, the benefits for an establishment can be significant. However, the potential pitfalls are just as considerable. For food managers, a thorough grasp of their state's licensing requirements and regulations is not just a matter of legal compliance; it's a critical component of running a successful, reputable, and safe establishment.

9.2 Safe Serving of Alcohol

In the world of food and beverage service, the ability to serve alcohol comes with both rewards and responsibilities. While the addition of alcoholic beverages can elevate the dining experience and increase an establishment's revenue, it also introduces potential risks.

Before delving into the practices of safe serving, it's essential to understand alcohol's effects on the human body. Alcohol depresses the central nervous system, impacting a person's motor skills, decision-making abilities, and reaction time. While some people might seem "tolerant" to alcohol's effects, no amount of regular drinking makes the body immune to its impacts.

Identification Checks: Ensuring that alcohol is not served to underage individuals is a primary concern. As of now, the legal drinking age in the USA is 21. Therefore, staff should be trained to diligently check IDs, recognizing valid identification and spotting fake ones. Some states even mandate electronic ID scanners for added accuracy.

Recognizing Intoxication: An essential skill for anyone serving alcohol is the ability to recognize signs of intoxication. Common symptoms include slurred speech, impaired coordination, aggressive behavior, and overly emotional reactions. Staff should be trained to spot these signs and take appropriate action, whether that means refusing service, offering water or food, or arranging for a safe way home for the patron.

Strategies to Prevent Overconsumption

Beyond just recognizing intoxication, establishments should have strategies in place to prevent it. This can include:

- Offering a variety of non-alcoholic beverages
- Encouraging food consumption alongside drinks
- Implementing a limit on the number of drinks served to an individual within a specified time
- Using standardized measurements for alcoholic drinks to ensure consistency

- Handling Refusals: There will be times when staff must refuse service to a patron, either because of age or visible intoxication. Employees should be trained on how to handle these situations delicately, avoiding confrontation. Clear communication, backed by management, is key.

Safe Transportation Options: Ensuring that patrons have a safe way home after consuming alcohol should be a priority. This might mean partnering with local taxi services, promoting ride-share apps, or even offering designated driver incentives.

Liabilities and Dram Shop Laws: Many states have "dram shop" laws, which can hold an establishment liable if they serve alcohol to someone clearly intoxicated, and that person subsequently causes harm or injury. Awareness and understanding of these laws are vital for any establishment serving alcohol.

Training Programs: As touched upon in the previous section, many states require formal training for servers and bartenders. Programs like TIPS (Training for Intervention Procedures) equip staff with the knowledge and skills needed to serve alcohol responsibly.

9.3 Addressing Overconsumption and Intoxication

Addressing overconsumption and intoxication in a hospitality setting is a delicate balance of ensuring patron safety, maintaining a positive establishment reputation, and avoiding legal liabilities. Given the potential consequences of overconsumption, both to the individual and to others, food managers must be well-equipped with knowledge and strategies to address these challenges effectively.

Overconsumption refers to the excessive intake of alcohol in a short period. It can lead to intoxication, impaired judgment, health risks, and in severe cases, alcohol poisoning. Recognizing overconsumption early is essential to prevent these potential outcomes.

Strategies to Mitigate Overconsumption

- Drink Pacing: Encourage servers to pace the drinks they serve. One standard drink per hour is a general guideline. This pacing allows the body's metabolism to process the alcohol and helps prevent rapid intoxication.

- Promote Food with Alcohol: Consuming food slows the absorption of alcohol in the bloodstream. Offering snacks or meals alongside drinks can mitigate the effects of alcohol.

- Provide Non-Alcoholic Alternatives: Offer an enticing range of non-alcoholic beverages for patrons who may want to alternate between alcoholic and non-alcoholic drinks.

- Awareness of Alcohol Content: Not all drinks are created equal. A cocktail may contain much more alcohol than a standard beer. Servers should be knowledgeable about the alcohol content in the beverages they serve and communicate this to patrons when necessary.

Addressing Intoxication

1. Empower Staff: All staff should be trained to recognize the signs of intoxication and feel empowered to refuse service when necessary. This decision should always be supported by management.
2. Engage in a Conversation: If a patron appears to be intoxicated, approach the situation with empathy. Engage them in a calm conversation, ask how they're feeling, and gently suggest they might want to take a break from drinking.
3. Offer Alternatives: Instead of just cutting off service, offer alternatives like water, coffee, or food. This approach can diffuse potential tensions and shows that the establishment cares about the patron's well-being.

4. Implement a Buddy System: Encourage groups to look out for one another. If one member of a party is overindulging, their friends or acquaintances might be the best people to intervene and persuade them to slow down or stop.

5. Have Security Measures in Place: In instances where patrons become aggressive or unruly due to intoxication, having security personnel on hand can help ensure the safety of both staff and other patrons.

Legal Implications and Responsibilities

- Dram Shop Liability: As previously mentioned, establishments can be held responsible for the actions of an intoxicated patron after they leave. This underscores the importance of responsible serving practices.

- Documentation: It's beneficial for establishments to document incidents related to overconsumption or intoxication. This can be vital for legal protection and also offers a chance for staff to review and learn from situations.

- Continued Training: Regulations and best practices can change. Regularly updating training programs ensures that staff remain knowledgeable and equipped to handle situations related to overconsumption and intoxication.

9.4 Preservation and Storage of Alcoholic Beverages

When it comes to the management of alcoholic beverages, ensuring their proper storage and conservation is of paramount importance. Not only does this practice affect the quality and taste of the drink, but it can also have implications for safety, cost management, and regulatory compliance. As with food items, alcohol requires specific conditions for optimal storage.

The proper storage of alcoholic beverages ensures:

- Maintenance of flavor and quality.
- Extended shelf life and minimized waste.
- Compliance with health and safety regulations.
- Preservation of investment, as some alcoholic beverages can be quite costly.

Basics of Storing Different Types of Alcohol

Wines:

- Red Wines: Ideally stored horizontally, especially if sealed with a cork, in a dark, cool place between 55°F and 65°F.
- White and Rosé Wines: Require cooler storage temperatures, typically between 40°F and 50°F.
- Champagnes and Sparkling Wines: Must be kept in a cooler environment, between 40°F and 45°F.

Beers:

Darker beers such as stouts or porters can be stored like red wines, but lighter beers like lagers or pilsners prefer colder storage, similar to white wines. Always keep beer away from direct sunlight.

Spirits and Liqueurs:

- Spirits (vodka, gin, whiskey, rum, etc.) are best stored upright in a cool, dark place. Unlike wines, they do not benefit from aging once bottled.
- Liqueurs, especially those that are cream-based, might require refrigeration after opening.
- Fortified Wines (like Sherry or Port) can benefit from cooler storage temperatures, similar to red wines, but do not need as precise temperature control.

Environmental Considerations

Light: Ultraviolet light can degrade and prematurely age alcoholic beverages. Dark bottles help protect contents, but storing in a dark environment is always best.

Vibration: Excessive vibration, especially for wines, can negatively impact their aging process. Ensure storage areas are free from constant vibrations.

Humidity: A relative humidity of about 60-70% is ideal for storing wine, especially with cork seals, to prevent them from drying out. Remember: excessive humidity can also be responsible for mold growth and a permanent damage to the label.

Inventory Rotation and Management

First-In, First-Out (FIFO): Like with food items, using a FIFO system ensures that older stock is used before newer stock, minimizing potential waste due to spoilage.

Regular Audits: Periodically checking inventory can help identify any bottles that might be nearing the end of their optimal storage life or any potential issues with storage conditions.

Special Considerations for Rare or Aged Alcohols

Climate-Controlled Storage: For particularly valuable or sensitive alcoholic beverages, investing in climate-controlled storage or specialized wine refrigerators can be beneficial.

Insurance: Especially for rare and expensive collections, considering insurance can protect the investment against potential loss.

Health and Safety Regulations

- Storage of alcohol must also consider safety regulations:

- Restrictions on Quantity: Some regions may have limits on the amount of alcohol a business can store on-premises.

- Secure Storage: Especially for establishments with extensive and valuable collections, secure storage can prevent theft and unauthorized access.

- Labeling and Record Keeping: Accurate records and labels can aid in inventory management and ensure compliance with regulatory bodies.

9.5 Staff Training on Alcohol Service

Staff training is not merely a recommendation; in many states, it's a legal requirement. Trained staff can:

- Prevent sales to underage patrons.
- Identify and manage intoxicated customers.
- Handle difficult situations tactfully, reducing the potential for escalation.
- Understand and respect local, state, and federal regulations.
- Enhance the customer's experience by offering knowledgeable service and recommendations.

Components of a Comprehensive Alcohol Service Training Program

1. Understanding Alcohol: This includes the effects of alcohol on the body, the factors that influence intoxication, and the basics of alcohol metabolism. A deeper understanding will help staff gauge the impact of drinks on patrons.

2. Checking Identification: Staff should be trained on how to properly check IDs to verify age, identify fake or altered IDs, and recognize IDs from different states or countries.

3. Recognizing Intoxication: It's essential to equip staff with the skills to identify signs of intoxication. This includes changes in behavior, slurred speech, impaired coordination, and overconfidence.

4. Handling Difficult Situations: This can range from refusing service to an intoxicated patron, dealing with aggressive behavior, or managing situations where a patron's safety might be compromised, such as ensuring they don't drive.

5. Legal Aspects: Staff should be made aware of the legal implications of over-serving, serving minors, and other potential violations. This includes both the consequences for the establishment and potential personal liabilities for the server.

6. Service Best Practices: Beyond safety considerations, training should include how to serve drinks correctly, including proper pouring techniques, understanding drink measurements, and offering non-alcoholic alternatives.

7. Cultural and Ethical Considerations: In a diverse society, understanding cultural differences related to alcohol consumption can be invaluable. This includes recognizing religious or cultural practices that might influence a patron's choice or behavior.

8. Emergency Procedures: Should an incident occur, staff must know how to respond, whether it's a medical emergency, a physical altercation, or any other unexpected event.

Regular Refresher Courses

It's not enough to train staff once and consider the task complete. Regular refresher courses ensure that staff remains updated with the latest regulations, practices, and challenges related to alcohol service. New scenarios or issues that have arisen in the establishment can be addressed in these sessions.

Conclusion: Preparing for the Path Ahead

As you come to the close of this comprehensive guide on the many facets of food management, it's imperative to recognize the depth and breadth of knowledge and responsibility the role demands. Food managers are entrusted not only with the safety and health of the consumers but also with the ethical and efficient operation of an establishment. The position is a unique blend of science, technique, ethics, and passion.

We have journeyed through the microscopic world of foodborne microorganisms and allergens, understanding their complexities and the illnesses they can cause. We've delved into the importance of personal hygiene, a cornerstone in preventing many foodborne illnesses. The intricate dance of purchasing, receiving, storing, preparing, and serving food safely was dissected, emphasizing the need for precision and vigilance at every step. Facility management, from maintaining cleanliness to thwarting pesky invaders, demonstrated the daily challenges a food manager might face.

Yet, it wasn't all about risks and regulations. We ventured into the art and science of advanced cooking techniques, from the precise nature of sous-vide cooking to the wonders of molecular gastronomy. The world of food is ever-evolving, and as a food manager, one is at the forefront of these culinary revolutions, merging tradition with innovation.

Equally important is the profound understanding and respect for dietary restrictions and food ethics. In today's globalized world, it's commonplace to cater to a diverse clientele, each with unique dietary requirements or preferences. Beyond serving, it's about respecting their choices, be it for health, religion, or ethics. Moreover, in an age where consumers are more aware and concerned about the origins of their food, ethical sourcing and understanding the intricacies of genetically modified foods have never been more crucial.

This guide aimed to equip you with the foundational knowledge necessary to embark on your journey toward becoming a certified food manager. But reading alone isn't enough. The real test of understanding and internalizing this information lies ahead.

Now, you stand at the precipice of the true challenge: the Food Manager Certification Exam. But fret not! Armed with the knowledge from this guide, you are well-prepared to face it head-on. The subsequent test preparations, accessible through the QR code, are designed to help you reinforce your learning, identify areas of improvement, and get a feel for the actual examination.

Before you proceed, take a moment to reflect on your journey thus far. The food industry, while rewarding, is fraught with challenges, but it is those very challenges that can mold you into an expert in the field. The responsibility is immense, but so is the potential for growth, innovation, and making a meaningful impact.

In conclusion, the road to becoming a certified food manager is demanding, but it is a path filled with opportunities for those passionate about food and dedicated to their craft. As you move towards the QR code and begin your test preparations, remember that every challenge is an opportunity in disguise. Embrace it, learn from it, and above all, enjoy the journey. The world of food awaits you with open arms, ready to be explored, respected, and celebrated.

Download All your Practice Tests With This QR Code or Follow This Link:

https://book-bonus.com/food-manager/

Made in the USA
Las Vegas, NV
03 January 2024

83814498R00069